ancient music in the pines

OSHO

DVD: *Zen Was Born In Laughter*, Copyright © 1987, 2007, OSHO International Foundation, Switzerland

This book is a transcript of a series of original talks by Osho given to a live audience.
The talks in this edition were previously published as *Ancient Music in the Pines*.
All of Osho's talks have been published in full as books, and are also available as original audio and/or video recordings.
Audio recordings and the complete text archive can be found via the online OSHO Library at www.osho.com
OSHO is a registered trademark of Osho International Foundation, www.osho.com/trademarks

Osho comments in this work on excerpts from the following works:

Zen and Japanese Culture by Daisetz T. Suzuki
Routledge & Kegan Paul Ltd, 1959; Broadway House, 68–74 Carter Lane, London EC4
© 1959 Bollingen Foundation Inc, New York, NY

Zen and Japanese Buddhism by Daisetz T. Suzuki
Published by Japan Travel Bureau Inc.; Maronuchi 1-Chome, Chiyodaku, Tokyo
© 1965 by Japan Travel Bureau, First. Ed. 1958, 2nd 1961, 3rd March 1965, 4th Oct. 1965

Zen: Poems, Prayers, Sermons, Anecdotes, Interviews edited/translated by Lucien Stryk and Takas
© 1963, 1965 by Lucien Stryk and Takashi Ikemoto, published by Doubleday Anchor Books
Doubleday & Company, Inc., Garden City, New York, USA (pages 116, 126)

OSHO MEDIA INTERNATIONAL

New York • London • Mumbai
an imprint of
OSHO INTERNATIONAL
www.osho.com/oshointernational

Distributed by Publishers Group Worldwide
www.pgw.com

Library of Congress Cataloging-in-Publication data is available

ISBN 13   978-0-9844444-2-7
ISBN 10   0-9844444-2-4
Also available as an eBook: ISBN 13   978-0-88050-205-4

Printed in China

10   9   8   7   6   5   4   3   2   1

Design by Bookcraft Ltd
Cover design by Terry Jeavons
Jacket image © Terry Jeavons

ancient music in the pines

in zen, mind suddenly stops

the way of effortless effort

Contents

Preface   6

Chapter 1   **Left brain, right brain inner conflict**   9

Chapter 2   **The meaning of maturity**   26

Chapter 3   **The halo of Yakushi-Buddha**   45

Chapter 4   **Be a light unto yourself**   60

Chapter 5   **The ultimate secrets of swordsmanship**   78

Chapter 6   **Madman and devotees**   94

Chapter 7   **The proper state of mind**   109

Chapter 8   **Life, death and love**   125

Chapter 9   **You have my marrow**   143

Preface

You may not know that the word meditation comes from the same root as medicine, medical, and the original meaning of the word was – a technique to become whole, a technique to become healthy. Medicine is medicinal, just like that, meditation is also medicinal. It makes you whole, integrated, healthy.

Pay attention, listen as meditatively as possible. When you listen meditatively you understand, when you listen concentratedly you learn. If you listen with concentration, you will gain knowledge, if you listen meditatively, you will lose knowledge. And the difference is very subtle.

When you listen attentively, attention means a tension – it means you are tense, too eager to learn, to absorb, to know. You are interested in knowledge, concentration is the way towards knowledge; a mind focused on one thing of course learns more.

Meditation is unfocused mind, you simply listen silently, not with a tension in the mind, not with an urge to know and learn, no, with total relaxation, in a let-go, in an opening of your being.

You listen, not to know, you simply listen to understand. These are different ways of listening.

If you are trying to know, then you are trying to memorize what I am saying; deep down you are repeating it, you are taking notes inside the mind, you are writing it in the world of your memories. You are interested in letting it become deeply rooted in you so you don't forget. Then it will become knowledge.

And the same seed could have become unlearning, understanding. Then you simply listen, you are not interested in accumulating it, you are not interested in writing it in your memory, in your mind. You simply listen open – as you listen to music, as you listen to birds singing in the trees, as you listen to wind passing through ancient pines, as you listen to the sound of water in a waterfall. There is nothing to remember, nothing to memorize. You don't listen with a parrot mind, you simply listen without any mind – the listening is beautiful, it is ecstatic, there is no goal in it, in itself it is ecstatic, it is blissful.

Listen meditatively, not with concentration. All schools, colleges, universities, teach concentration, because the goal is to memorize. Here the goal is not to memorize, the goal is not to learn at all, the goal is to unlearn.

Listen silently, and don't think that you will forget. There is no need to remember; only that which is rubbish has to be remembered, because you go on forgetting it.

Whenever you hear the truth there is no need to remember it, because it cannot be forgotten. You may not be able to remember the words but you will remember the essence – and that will not be part of your memory, it will be part of your being.

Knowledge is a doing, it is a conflict, struggle, what Darwin calls "survival of the fittest." It is fighting with nature, it is a constant war of man against the whole. Foolish – but it is there.

When you want to learn something you are in fact trying to learn to *do* something. All knowledge is pragmatic, practical, you will transform it into your practice, you will do something with it. Otherwise you will say, Why learn? What is the point? You learn it as a utility.

That's why in a pragmatic, empirical world arts by and by disappear. Nobody wants to listen to poetry, nobody wants to listen to music, because the question is: What can you *do* with it? Can you make money out of it? Can you become powerful out of it? What can you do? Can you repair a car by listening to music? Can you make a house? No, it cannot be used, music is non-utilitarian, it has no utility – and that's the beauty of it.

Whole life is non-utilitarian, it has no purpose, it is not going anywhere. It is simply being here, it is not going anywhere. It has no goal to achieve, it has no destiny. It is a cosmic play, what Hindus call *leela*, a play, just children playing with no goal in view. Playing itself is the goal, they are enjoying it, they are delighting in it, they are happy – finished!

Learning is always with the view to do something. It is a technique towards becoming a great doer. If you know more, you can do more. Then what will unlearning do? It will make you a non-doer.

By and by you will not know anything, you will not be able to do. By and by as knowledge disappears from you, doing will also disappear. You will become *being*, you will *be*, but you will not be a doer. I don't mean that you will not do anything – even a Buddha has to beg, even Lao Tzu must have tried ways and means to find bread and butter and things like that; when it was raining he must have found a shelter – he lived a long life, and he lived a very healthy life. No, I don't mean that you don't do, I mean you become a non-doer. Things start happening. You don't do them, they happen. The doer, the manipulator, goes, dissolves, disappears – and with the doer gone, the ego is no longer found.

Chapter 1

Left Brain, Right Brain Inner Conflict

Gosa Hoyen used to say, "When people ask me what Zen is like I tell them this story:
Noticing that his father was growing old, the son of a burglar asked his father to teach him the trade so that he could carry on the family business after his father had retired. The father agreed, and that night they broke into a house together.
Opening a large chest the father told his son to go in and pick out the clothing. As soon as the boy was inside, the father locked the chest and then made a lot of noise so that the whole house was aroused. Then he slipped quietly away.
Locked inside the chest the boy was angry, terrified, and puzzled as to how he was going to get out. Then an idea flashed to him – he made a noise like a cat.
The family told a maid to take a candle and examine the chest. When the lid was unlocked the boy jumped out, blew out the candle, pushed his way past the astonished maid, and ran out. The people ran after him.
Noticing a well by the side of the road the boy threw in a large stone, then hid in the darkness. The pursuers gathered around the well trying to see the burglar drowning himself.
When the boy got home he was very angry at his father and he tried to tell him the story. But the father said, 'Don't bother to tell me the details. You are here – you have learned the art.'"

Being is one, the world is many, and between the two is the divided mind, the dual mind. It is just like a big tree, an ancient oak: the trunk is lone, then the tree divides into two main branches, the main bifurcation from which a thousand and one bifurcations of branches grow.

The being is just like the trunk of the tree: one, non-dual. The mind is the first bifurcation where the tree divides into two, becomes dual, becomes dialectical: thesis and antithesis, man and woman, yin and yang, day and night, God and Devil, Yoga and Zen.

All the dualities of the world are basically in the duality of the mind, and below the duality is oneness of being. If you slip below, underneath the duality, you will find one – call it God, call it nirvana or whatsoever you like. If you go higher through the duality, you come to the many million-fold world.

This is one of the most basic insights to be understood: that mind is not one. Hence whatsoever you see through the mind becomes two. It is just like a white ray entering a prism: it is immediately divided into seven colors and the rainbow is created. Before it entered the prism it was one; through the prism it is divided and the white color disappears into seven colors of the rainbow.

The world is a rainbow, the mind is a prism, and the being is the white ray.

Modern research has come to a very significant fact, one of the most significant achieved in this century, and that is that you don't have one mind, you have two minds. Your brain is divided into two hemispheres: the right hemisphere and the left hemisphere. The right hemisphere is joined with the left hand, and the left hemisphere is joined with the right hand – crosswise. The right hemisphere is intuitive, illogical, irrational, poetic, platonic, imaginative, romantic, mythical, religious; the left hemisphere is logical, rational, mathematical, Aristotelian, scientific, calculative. These two hemispheres are constantly in conflict. The basic politics of the world is within you, the greatest politics of the world is within you. You may not be aware of it but once you become aware, the real thing to be done is somewhere between these two minds.

The left hand is concerned with the right hemisphere that is intuition, imagination, myth, poetry, religion. The left hand is very much condemned. The society is of those who are right-handed; right-handed means left hemisphere. Ten percent of children are born left-handed but they are forced to be right-handed. Children who are born left-handed are basically irrational, intuitive, non-mathematical, non-Euclidian. They are dangerous to the society; the society forces them in every way to become right-handed. It is not just a question of hands, it is a question of inner politics: the left-handed child functions through the right hemisphere. That, society cannot allow, it is dangerous; he has to be stopped before things go too far.

It is suspected that in the beginning the proportion must have been fifty-fifty: left-handed children fifty percent and right-handed children fifty percent. But the right-handed party has ruled so long that by and by the proportion has fallen to ten percent and ninety percent. Even amongst you here, many will be left-handed but you may not be aware of it. You may be writing with the right hand and do your work with the right hand, but in your childhood you may have been forced to be right-handed. This is a trick, because once you become right-handed your left hemisphere starts functioning. The left hemisphere is reason, the right hemisphere is beyond reason. Its functioning is not mathematical – it functions in flashes, it is intuitive, very graceful, but irrational.

The left-handed minority is the most oppressed minority in the world, even more than the negroes, even more than the poor people. Now if you understand this division you can understand many things. The bourgeoisie and the proletariat: the proletariat is always functioning through the right hemisphere of the brain; poor people are more intuitive. Go to primitive people – they are more intuitive. The poorer the person, the less intellectual. And that may be the cause of his being poor. Because he is less intellectual he cannot compete in the world of reason: he is less articulate as far as language is concerned, reason is concerned, calculation is concerned; he is almost a fool. That may be the cause of his being poor.

And the rich person is functioning through the left hemisphere of the brain: he is more calculative, arithmetical in everything; cunning, clever, logical, planning. That may be the reason why he is rich.

Now the proletariat and the bourgeoisie cannot disappear through communist revolutions, no, because the communist revolution is by the same kind of people. The czar ruled Russia; he ruled it through the left hemisphere of the mind. Then he was replaced by Lenin who is again of the same type. Then Lenin is replaced by Stalin who is even more the same type. The revolution is false because deep down the same type of people are ruling: the ruler and the ruled remain the same; the ruled are of the right-sided hemisphere. So whatsoever you do in the outside world makes no difference really; it is superficial.

The same applies to men and women. Women are right-hemisphere people, men are left-hemisphere people. Men have ruled women for centuries. Now a few women are revolting, but the amazing thing is that these are the same type of women. In fact they are just like men: rational, argumentative, Aristotelian.

It is possible that one day, just as the communist revolution has succeeded in Russia and China, one day somewhere – maybe in America – women can succeed and overthrow men. But by the time women succeed, the women will no longer be women; by that time they will have become left-hemisphered – because to fight one has to be calculative, and to fight with men you have to be like men, aggressive.

That very aggressiveness is shown all over the world in women's liberation. Women who have become part of that liberation movement are very aggressive; they are losing all grace, all that comes out of intuition – because if you have to fight with men you have to learn the same trick, if you have to fight with men you have to fight with the same techniques. Fighting with anybody is very dangerous because you become like your enemy.

That is one of the greatest problems of human history. Once you fight with somebody, by and by you have to use the same technique and the same way. The enemy may be defeated, but by the time he is defeated you have become your own enemy. Stalin is more czar-like than any czar, more violent than any czar. Of course, it has to be so: to overthrow czars, very violent people are needed, more violent than the czar himself. Only they will become the revolutionaries, only they will come out on top. By the time they reach there, they have become czars themselves, and society continues in the same way. Just superficial things change; deep down the same conflict remains.

The conflict is in man. Unless it is resolved there, it cannot be resolved anywhere else. The politics is within you, it is between your two parts of the mind. A very small bridge exists. If that bridge is broken through some accident, through some physiological defect or something else, the person becomes split, the person becomes two persons and the phenomenon of schizophrenia or split personality happens. If the bridge is broken — and the bridge is very fragile — then you become two, you behave like two persons. In the morning you are very loving, very beautiful, in the evening you are very angry, absolutely different. And you don't remember your morning — how can you remember? — another mind was functioning and the person becomes two persons. If this bridge is strengthened so much that the two minds disappear as two and become one, then integration, then crystallization arises.

What George Gurdjieff used to call the crystallization of being is nothing but these two minds becoming one, the meeting of the male and the female within, the meeting of yin and yang, the meeting of the left and right, the meeting of logic and illogic, the meeting of Plato and Aristotle.

If you can understand this basic bifurcation in your tree of life then you can understand all the conflict that goes on around you and inside you.

Let me tell you an anecdote:

Among the Germans, Berlin is considered to be the very epitome of Prussian brusqueness and efficiency, while Vienna is the essence of Austrian charm and slipshoddiness.

There is the tale of a Berliner visiting Vienna who was lost and in need of directions. What would such a Berliner do? He grabbed at the lapel of the first passing Viennese and barked out, "The Post Office, where is it?"

The startled Viennese carefully detached the other's fist, smoothed his lapel and said in a gentle manner, "Sir, would it not have been more delicate of you to have approached me politely and to have said, 'Sir, if you have a moment and happen to know, could you please direct me to the Post Office?'"

The Berliner stared in astonishment for a moment, then growled, "I would rather be lost!" and stomped away.

That very same Viennese was visiting Berlin later that year and it turned out that now it was he who had to search for the Post Office. Approaching a Berliner he said politely, "Sir, if you have a moment and happen to know, could you please direct me to the Post Office?"

With machine-like rapidity the Berliner replied, "About face, two blocks forward, sharp turn right, one block forward, cross a street, half turn on the right, walk left over railroad tracks, pass newsstand into Post Office lobby."

The Viennese, more bewildered than enlightened, nevertheless murmured, "A thousand thanks, kind sir," whereupon the Berliner snatched furiously at the other's lapel and shouted, "Never mind the thanks, repeat the instructions!"

The male mind, the Berliner; the female mind, the Viennese ... The female mind has a grace, the male mind has efficiency. And of course, in the long run, if there is a constant fight, the grace is bound to be defeated. The efficient mind will win because the world understands the language of mathematics, not of love. But the moment your efficiency wins over your grace, you have lost something tremendously valuable, you have lost contact with your own being. You may become very efficient but you will no longer be a real person. You will become a machine, a robot-like thing.

Because of this there is constant conflict between man and woman. They cannot remain separate; they have to get into relationship again and again. But they cannot remain together either. The fight is not outside, the fight is within you. And this is my understanding: unless you have resolved your inner fight between the left and the right hemispheres, you will never be able to be peacefully in love, never – because the inner fight will be reflected outside. If you are fighting inside and you are identified with the left hemisphere, the reason hemisphere, and continuously trying to overpower the right hemisphere, you will try to do the same with the woman you fall in love with. If the woman is continuously fighting her own reason inside, she will continuously fight the man she loves.

All relationships – almost all, the exceptions are negligible, can be left out of account – become ugly. In the beginning they are beautiful. In the beginning you don't show the reality, in the beginning you pretend. Once the relationship settles and you relax, your inner conflict bubbles up and starts being mirrored in your relationship – then fights, then a thousand and one ways of nagging each other, destroying each other. Hence the attraction for homosexuality: whenever a society has become too much – because at least a man in love with a man is not that much in conflict. The love relationship may not be very satisfying, may not lead to tremendous bliss and orgasmic moments, but at least it is not as ugly as the relationship between a man and a woman. Women become lesbians whenever the conflict becomes too much, because at least the love relationship between two women is not so deep in conflict. The same meets the same, they can understand each other.

Yes, understanding is possible, but the attraction is lost, the polarity is lost. It is at a very great cost. Understanding is possible, but the whole tension, the challenge, is lost. And if you choose challenge, then comes conflict, because the real problem is somewhere within you. Unless you have settled, come to a deep harmony between your female and male mind, you will not be able to love.

People come to me and they ask how to go deep in a relationship. I tell them, "First, go deeply into meditation. Unless you are resolved within yourself you will create more problems than you already have. If you move in relationship all your problems will be multiplied." Just watch. The greatest and the most beautiful thing on earth is love, but can you find anything more ugly, more hell-creating?

Mulla Nasruddin once told me, "Well, I've been putting off the evil day for months, but I have got to go this time."

"Dentist or doctor?" I enquired.

"Neither," he said, "I am getting married."

People go on avoiding marriage, people go on putting it off. When some day they find it impossible to get out of it, only then do they relax.

Where is the problem? Why are people so afraid of getting deeply involved? Involvement immediately creates fear; commitment immediately creates fear – and the modern man wants to have sex but no love.

A woman told me that she wants sex only with strangers. Traveling in a train, meeting a stranger, that's okay, but not even with someone who is friendly or familiar.

I asked, "Why?"

She said that once you make love to someone who is known to you, some involvement starts. In a train, on a journey, you meet, make love – you don't know even what the other person's name is, who he is, from where he comes. You get down when your station comes and he moves away, forgotten forever. He leaves no scratch, you remain completely clean. You come out of it completely clean and unscratched.

I can understand. This is the difficulty of the whole modern mind. All relationships are becoming casual by and by. People are afraid of any sort of commitment because they have come to know at least one thing out of bitter experience: whenever you become too much related, the reality erupts and your inner conflicts start being reflected by the other. And then life becomes ugly, horrible, intolerable.

It happened once: I was sitting with a few friends in a university campus ground. One of the professors said, "On the day my wedding occurred ... "

But the other professor stopped him immediately and said, "Pardon the correction, but affairs such as marriages, receptions, dinners, and things of that nature, take place. It is only calamities which occur. Do you see the distinction? Please don't say, 'The day my marriage occurred' or 'The day my wedding occurred.'"

The other was a professor of language and of course he was right. But the first man said, "Yes, many, many things ... " and again started. " ... and as I was saying, the day my wedding occurred, it was a calamity."

If you are outside it, it may look like a beautiful oasis in the desert, but as you come closer the oasis starts drying and disappearing. Once you are caught in it, it is an imprisonment. But remember, the imprisonment doesn't come from the other, it comes from within you.

If the left-hemisphere brain goes on dominating you, you will live a very successful life, so successful that by the time you are forty you will have ulcers, by the time you are forty-five you will have at least one or two heart-attacks, by the time you are fifty you will be almost dead — but successfully dead. You may become a great scientist but you will never become a great being. You may accumulate enough wealth but you will lose all that is of worth. You may conquer the whole world like an Alexander but your own inner territory will remain unconquered.

There are many attractions of following the left-hemisphere brain, that is the worldly brain. It is more concerned with things: cars, houses, money, power, prestige. That is the orientation of the man who in India we call a *grihastha*, a householder.

The right-hemisphere brain is the orientation of a sannyasin, one who is more interested in his own inner being, his inner peace, his blissfulness, and is less concerned about things. If they come easily, good; if they don't come that too is good. He is more concerned with the moment, less concerned with the future; more concerned with the poetry of life, less concerned with the arithmetic of it.

I have heard an anecdote:

Finkelstein had made a huge killing at the races and Muscovitz, quite understandably, was envious.

"How did you do it, Finkelstein?" he demanded.

"Easy," said Finkelstein, "it was a dream."

"A dream?"

"Yes. I had figured out a three-horse parlay, but I was not sure about the third horse. Then, the night before I dreamed that an angel was standing at the head of my bed and kept saying, 'Blessings on you, Finkelstein, seven times seven blessings on you.' When I woke up I realized that seven times seven is forty-eight and that horse number forty-eight was Heavenly Dream. I made Heavenly Dream the third horse in my parlay and I just cleaned up, simply cleaned up."

Muscovitz said, "But Finkelstein, seven times seven is forty-nine!"

And Finkelstein said, "So you are a mathematician!"

There is a way to follow life through arithmetic, and there is another way to follow life through dreams and visions. They are totally different.

Just the other day somebody asked, "Are there ghosts, fairies, and things like that?" Yes, there are – if you move through the right-hemisphere brain there are, if you move through the left-hemisphere brain there are not. All children are right-hemisphered: they see ghosts and fairies all around. But you go on talking to them and putting them in their places and saying to them, "Nonsense! You are stupid. Where is the fairy? There is nothing, just a shadow." By and by you convince the child, the helpless child; by and by you convince him and he moves from right-hemisphered orientation to left-hemisphered orientation. He has to; he has to live in your world. He has to forget his dreams, he has to forget all myths, he has to forget all poetry – he has to learn mathematics. Of course he becomes efficient in mathematics and becomes almost crippled and paralyzed in life. Existence goes on getting farther and farther away and he becomes just a commodity in the market. His whole life becomes just rubbish, but of course, valuable in the eyes of the world.

A sannyasin is one who lives through the imagination, who lives through the dreaming quality of his mind, who lives through poetry, who poeticizes about life, who looks through visions. Then trees are greener than they look to you, then birds are more beautiful, then everything takes a luminous quality. Ordinary pebbles become diamonds, ordinary rocks are no longer ordinary – nothing is ordinary. If you look from the right hemisphere, everything becomes divine, sacred. Religion is from the right hemisphere.

A man was sitting with his friend in a cafeteria drinking tea. He studied his cup and said with a sigh, "Ah, my friend, life is like a cup of tea."

The other considered that for a moment and then said, "But why? Why is life like a cup of tea?"

The first man replied, "How should I know? Am I a philosopher?"

The right-hemisphere brain only makes statements about facts, it cannot give you reasons. If you ask, "Why?" it can only remain silent, there comes no response from it. If you are walking and you see a lotus flower and you say, "Beautiful!" and somebody says, "Why?" what will you do? You will say, "How am I to know? Am I a philosopher?" It is a simple statement, a very simple statement, in itself total, complete. There is no reason behind it and no result beyond it; it is a simple statement of fact.

Read the Upanishads – they are simple statements of facts. They say, "Godliness is." Don't ask why, or they will say, "Are we philosophers? How are we to know?

Godliness is." They say godliness is beautiful, they say godliness is near, closer than your heart – but don't ask why, they are not philosophers.

Look at the gospels and the statements of Jesus: they are simple. He says, "My God is in heaven. I am his son, he is my father. Don't ask why." He will not be able to prove it in a court, he will simply say, "I know." If you ask him by whom he has been told, by what authority he says these things, he will say, "It is by my own authority. I have no other authority." That is the problem when a man like Jesus moves in the world: the rational mind cannot understand. He was not crucified for any other reason – he was crucified by the left hemisphere because he was a right-hemisphere man. He was crucified because of the inner conflict.

Lao Tzu says, "The whole world seems to be clever, only I am muddle-headed. The whole world seems to be certain, only I am confused and hesitant." He is a right-hemisphered man.

The right hemisphere is the hemisphere of poetry and love. A great shift is needed and that shift is the inner transformation. Yoga is an effort to reach the one-ness of being through the left hemisphere, using logic, mathematics, science and trying to go beyond. Zen is just the opposite: the aim is the same but Zen uses the right hemisphere to go beyond. Both can be used, but to follow Yoga is a very, very long path. It is almost an unnecessary struggle because you are trying to reach from reason to super-reason, which is more difficult. Zen is easier because it is an effort to reach super-reason from irreason. Irreason is almost like super-reason – there are no barriers. Yoga is like penetrating a wall. And Zen is like opening a door – the door may not be closed at all, you just push it a little and it opens.

Now the story ... It is one of the most beautiful among Zen anecdotes. Zen people talk through stories. They have to talk through stories because they cannot create theories and doctrines, they can only tell stories. They are great storytellers. Jesus goes on talking in parables, Buddha goes on talking in parables, Sufi mystics go on talking in parables – it is not coincidental. The story, the parable, the anecdote, is the way of the right hemisphere. Logic, argument, proof, syllogism, is the way of the left hemisphere.

Listen to it ...

Gosa Hoyen used to say, "When people ask me what Zen is like
I tell them this story ... "

This story really tells what Zen is like without defining. It indicates. A definition is not possible because Zen, in its basic quality, is indefinable. You can taste it but you cannot define it, you can live it but language is not sufficient to say it, you can show it but you cannot say it. But through a story the quality can be transferred a little bit. And this story really indicates perfectly the quality of what Zen is like. This is just a gesture. Don't make it a definition, don't philosophize around it. Let it be like lightning – a flash of understanding. It is not going to increase your knowledge but it can give you a shift, a jerk, a change of gestalt. You can be thrown from one corner of the mind to another – and that is the whole point of the story.

Noticing that his father was growing old, the son of a burglar asked his father to teach him the trade so that he could carry on the family business after his father had retired.

Now the trade of a burglar is not a scientific thing, it is an art. Burglars are as much born as poets; you cannot learn, learning won't help. If you learn you will be caught – because then the police know more than you, they have accumulated centuries of learning. A burglar is a born burglar: he lives through intuition – it is a knack – he lives through hunches. A burglar is feminine; he is not a businessman, he is a gambler. He risks all for almost nothing; his whole trade is of danger and risk.

It is just like a religious man. Zen people say that religious people are also like burglars: in search of truth, they are also burglars. There is no way to reach truth through logic or reason or accepted society, culture, civilization. They break the wall somewhere, they enter from the back door. If in the daylight it is not allowed, they enter in the dark. If it is not possible to follow the crowd on the superhighway, they make their own individual paths in the forest. Yes, there is a certain similarity. You can reach truth only if you are a burglar – an artist of how to steal the fire, how to steal the treasure.

The father was going to retire and the son asked, "Before you retire teach me your trade."

The father agreed, and that night they broke into a house together.
Opening a large chest the father told his son to go in and pick out the clothing.
As soon as the boy was inside, the father locked the chest and then made a lot of noise so that the whole house was aroused. Then he slipped quietly away.

He must have been a real master, no ordinary burglar.

Locked inside the chest the boy was angry, terrified, and puzzled ...

Of course, naturally! What type of teaching was this? He had been thrown into a dangerous situation. But that is the only way to teach something of the unknown, that is the only way to teach something of the right-hemisphere brain. The left hemisphere can be taught in schools: learning is possible, discipline is possible, gradual courses are possible. Then by and by, moving from one class to another, you become masters of art and science and so many things. But there cannot be any schools for the right hemisphere: it is intuitive; it is not gradual, it is sudden. It is like a flash, a lightning in the dark night. If it happens, it happens, if it doesn't happen, it doesn't happen – nothing can be done about it. You can only leave yourself in a certain situation where there is more possibility for it to happen. That's why I say the old man must have been a real master.

Locked inside the chest the boy was angry, terrified, and puzzled ...

These are the three states your reason will pass through. In all my meditations the same is being done to you. Locked in a chest, with the key thrown away, first you feel angry. Many sannyasins come to me and they say they feel very angry with me. I can understand; it is natural: I am forcing them into situations where their old mind cannot function. That is the root cause of anger. They simply feel impotent, their old mind cannot function, they cannot make anything out of it: "What is happening?" And when you feel a situation where your mind is simply useless, you feel angry against me, angry and then terrified. Then one understands the whole situation and all that you have learned seems simply useless; hence fear.

Now there was no logical way to get out of that chest: it was locked from the outside, the father had made a noise and the whole house was awake, people were moving around, searching, and the father had escaped. Now is there any logical way to get out of this chest? Logic simply fails, reason is of no use. What can you think? Mind suddenly stops – and that is what the father is doing, that is what it is all about. He is trying to force the son into such a situation where the logical mind stops, because a burglar does not need a logical mind. If he follows a logical mind he will be caught sooner or later by the police because they also follow the same logic.

It happened in the Second World War ...

For three years Adolf Hitler continued to win, and the reason was that he was illogical. All the other countries that were fighting with him were fighting logically. Of course, they had a great science of war, military training, this and that, and they had experts who would say, "Now, Hitler is going to attack from this side." And if Hitler was also in his senses he would have done that because that was the weakest point in the enemy's defense. Of course the enemy has to be attacked where he is the weakest, it is logical. So they were expecting Hitler at the weakest point, they were gathering around the weakest point and he would hit anywhere, unpredictably. He would not even follow his own generals' advice.

He had an astrologer who would suggest where to attack. Now this is something never done before: a war is not run by astrologers. Once Churchill understood, once the spies came with the report that they were not going to win with this man because he was absolutely illogical, that a foolish astrologer who didn't know anything about war, who had never been on the front, was deciding things and deciding by the stars – what have stars got to do with a war going on, on the earth?

So Churchill immediately appointed a royal astrologer to the king and they started following the royal astrologer. Then things started falling in line, because now two fools were predicting. Things became easier.

If a burglar is going to follow Aristotle he will be caught sooner or later because the same Aristotelian logic is followed by the police.

Just a few days ago, Vedanta did a beautiful thing: he escaped with the ashram jeep. Of course the police had to be informed. Everybody was expecting that he would go towards Chanda, because he had been saying that he wanted to go to Chanda and reopen an old ashram which used to be there – Kailash. Had he gone towards there the police may not have followed him, but the police were thinking logically and they said, "If he had been saying that he was going towards Chanda he will not go to Chanda now because he will be afraid he will be caught on that road. He is not going there." So they were not worried about that road and, of course, Vedanta was caught in Lonavala. He was going towards Mumbai, but the police also followed the same logic.

If you go through logic, then anybody who follows the logical method can catch you anywhere. A burglar has to be unpredictable, logic is not possible. He has to be illogical, so much so that nobody can predict him. But illogic is possible only if your whole energy moves through the right hemisphere.

Locked inside the chest the boy was angry, terrified, and puzzled as to how he was going to get out.

"How?" is a logical question, hence he was terrified because there was no way, the "how" was simply impotent. Then an idea flashed to him. Now this is a shift: only in dangerous situations where the left hemisphere cannot function does it allow the right hemisphere to have its say as a last resort. When it cannot function, when it feels that now there is no go, now it is defeated, then: "Why not give a chance to the oppressed, to the imprisoned part of the mind? Give that too a chance. Maybe ... And there can be no harm!"

Suddenly ...

Then an idea flashed to him – he made a noise like a cat.

Now this is not logical. Making a noise like a cat is simply an absurd idea. But it worked.

The family told a maid to take a candle and examine the chest.
When the lid was unlocked the boy jumped out, blew out the candle,
pushed his way past the astonished maid, and ran out. The people
ran after him.
Noticing a well by the side of the road the boy threw in a large
stone, then hid in the darkness. The pursuers gathered around the
well trying to see the burglar drowning himself.

This too is not of the logical mind because the logical mind needs time. The logical mind needs time to proceed, to think, to argue this way and that, all the alternatives – and there are a thousand and one alternatives. When you are in a situation where there is no time to think, if people are pursuing you, how can you think? Thinking is good when you are sitting in an armchair. With your closed eyes you can philosophize and think and argue, for this and against that, pros and cons, but when people are pursuing you and your life is in danger you have no time to think – one lives in the moment, one simply becomes spontaneous.

It is not that he decided to throw the stone, it simply happened. It was not a conclusion, he was not thinking about doing it, he simply found himself doing it. He threw a stone in the well and hid himself in the darkness. The pursuers stopped, thinking the burglar had drowned himself in the well.

When the boy got home he was very angry at his father and he tried
to tell him the story. But the father said, 'Don't bother to tell me the
details. You are here – you have learned the art.'

What is the point of telling the details? They are useless. Details are useless as far as intuition is concerned because intuition is never a repetition. Details are meaningful as far as logic is concerned. So logical people go on into minute details so that if again the same situation happens they will be in control and they will know what to do.

But in the life of a burglar the same situation never happens again. And also in real life the same situation never happens again. If you have conclusions in your mind you will become almost dead, you will not be responding. In life, response, not reaction is needed: you have to act out of nowhere, with no conclusions inside. With no center you have to act; you have to act into the unknown from the unknown.

And this is what Goso Hoyen used to say when people asked him what Zen is like. He would tell this story.

Zen is exactly like burglary. It is an art, it is not a science; it is feminine, it is not male it is not aggressive; it is receptive, it is not a well-planned methodology; it is a spontaneity. It has nothing to do with theories, hypotheses, doctrines, scriptures – it has to do with only one thing, and that is awareness.

What happened in that moment when the boy was inside the chest? In such a danger you cannot be sleepy. In such a danger your consciousness becomes very sharp. It has to: life is at stake, you are totally awake. That's how one should be totally awake each moment. And when you are totally awake, this shift happens: from the left hemisphere the energy moves to the right hemisphere. Whenever you are alert you become intuitive; flashes come to you, flashes from the unknown, out of the blue. You may not follow them, but then you will miss much.

In fact all the great discoveries in science also come from the right hemisphere, not from the left. You must have heard about Madame Curie, the only woman who got a Nobel Prize ...

She had been working hard for three years on a certain mathematical problem but could not solve it. She worked hard, argued from this way and that, but there was no way.

One night, tired, exhausted, she fell asleep; while she was falling asleep then too she was trying to solve the problem. In the night she awoke, walked, wrote the answer on some paper, came back and went to sleep.

In the morning she found the answer there on the table. She could not believe who had done it! Nobody could do it! The servant? – you could not expect him to do it, he did not know anything about mathematics. She remembered well that the night before she had tried her best and could not do it. What had happened? Then she tried to remember – because the handwriting was hers. She tried to remember ... and then a faint remembrance came, as if in a dream she had walked to the table and written.

From where had this answer come? It could not be from the left hemisphere; the left had been working hard for three years. And there was no process on the paper, just the conclusion. If it had come from the left there would have been a process, it goes step by step. But this was like a flash – the same kind of flash that had happened to the boy in the chest. The left hemisphere, tired, exhausted, helpless, sought the help of the right hemisphere.

Whenever you are in such a corner where your logic fails, don't be desperate, don't become hopeless. Those moments may prove the greatest blessings in your life because those are the moments that the left allows the right to have its way. Then the feminine part, the receptive part, gives you an idea. If you follow it many doors will be opened. But it is possible you may miss it; you may say, "What nonsense!"

This boy could have missed because the idea was not very normal, regular, logical. Make a noise like a cat? For what? He could have asked, "Why?" and then he would have missed. But he could not ask because the situation was such that there was no other way. So he thought, "Let us try. What is wrong in it?" He used the clue.

The father was right. He said, "Don't go into details. They are not important. You are back home; you have learned the art."

The whole art is how to function from the feminine part of your mind, because the feminine is joined with the whole and the male is not joined with the whole. The male is aggressive, the male is constantly in struggle; the feminine is constantly in surrender, in deep trust. Hence the feminine body is so beautiful, so round. There is a deep trust and a deep harmony with nature. A woman lives in deep surrender; a man is constantly fighting, angry, doing this and that, trying to prove something, trying to reach somewhere. A woman is happy, not trying to reach anywhere.

Ask women if they would like to go to the moon: they will simply be amazed. "For what? What is the point? Why take such trouble? The home is perfectly good." The woman is not interested in what is happening in Vietnam and what is happening in Korea and what is happening in Israel. She is at the most interested in what is happening in the neighborhood, at the most interested in who has fallen in love with whom, who has escaped with whom – in gossips, not in politics. She is more interested in the immediate, the herenow. That gives her a harmony, a grace. Man is constantly trying to prove something, and if you want to prove of course you have to fight and compete and accumulate.

Once a woman tried to get Dr. Johnson to talk with her but he seemed to take very little notice of her.

"Why, doctor," she said archly, "I believe you prefer the company of men to that of women."

"Madam," replied Johnson, "I am very fond of the company of ladies. I like their beauty, I like their delicacy, I like their vivacity, and I like their silence."

Man has been forcing woman to be silent, not only outside, also inside – forcing the feminine part to keep quiet. Just watch within you. If the feminine part says something you immediately jump upon it and you say, "Logical? Absurd!"

People come to me and they say, "The heart says we would like to become sannyasins but the head says no" – Dr. Johnson, trying to keep the woman silent! The heart is feminine.

You miss much in your life because the head goes on talking; it does not allow. And the only quality in the head is that it is more articulate, cunning, dangerous, violent. Because of its violence it has become the leader inside, and that inside leadership has become an outside leadership for man. Man has dominated women in the outside world also – the grace is dominated by violence.

I was invited to a school for a certain function. There was a rally of school-children and in the rally the procession had been arranged according to height, the shortest first up to the tallest. But the pattern was broken, I noticed, by the first boy heading the procession. He was a gangling youth who looked a head taller than the rest.

"Why is he at the front?" I asked a young girl, "Is he the leader of the school, the captain, or something like that?"

"No," she whispered, "he pinches."

The male mind goes on pinching, creating trouble. Troublemakers become leaders. In schools, all wise teachers choose the greatest troublemakers as captains of the class and the school – the troublemakers, the criminals. Once they are in a powerful post, their whole energy for making trouble becomes helpful for the teacher. The same ones start creating discipline.

Just watch the politicians in the world: when one party is in power the opposite party goes on creating trouble in the country. They are the law-breakers, the revolutionaries. And the party which is in power goes on creating discipline. Once they are thrown out of power, they will create trouble. And once the opposite party comes into power, they become the guardians of discipline. They are all troublemakers.

The male mind is a troublemaking phenomenon, hence it overpowers, it dominates. But deep down, although you may attain power you miss life – and deep down, the feminine mind continues. And unless you fall back to the feminine and you surrender, unless your resistance and struggle become surrender you will not know what real life and the celebration of it is.

I have heard one anecdote:

An American scientist once visited the offices of the great Nobel Prize-winning physicist, Niels Bohr, in Copenhagen, and was amazed to find that over his desk was a horseshoe, securely nailed to the wall with the open end up in the approved manner so it would catch the good luck and not let it spill out.

The American said with a nervous laugh, "Surely you don't believe the horseshoe will bring you good luck, do you, Professor Bohr? After all, as a level-headed scientist ... "

Bohr chuckled, "I believe in no such thing, my good friend, not at all. I am scarcely likely to believe in such foolish nonsense. However, I am told that a horseshoe will bring you good luck whether you believe in it or not."

Look a little deeper, and just underneath your logic you will find fresh waters of intuition, fresh waters of trust flowing.

Yoga is a way to use reason to reach truth – of course very difficult, and the longest path. If you follow Patanjali you are trying to do that which can happen without doing; you are trying hard to do something which can happen right now without any effort. You are trying to pull yourself by shoe-strings – to pull yourself up.

Zen is the way of the spontaneous, effortless effort, the way of intuition.

A Zen master, Ikkyu, a great poet, has said,

I can see clouds a thousand miles away,
hear ancient music in the pines.

This is what Zen is all about. You cannot see clouds a thousand miles away with the logical mind. The logical mind is like a glass, too dirty, much too covered with the dust of ideas, theories, doctrines. But you can see clouds a thousand miles away with the pure glass of intuition, with no thoughts, just pure awareness. The mirror is clean and the clarity supreme.

You cannot hear ancient music in the pines with the ordinary logical mind. How can you hear the ancient music? Music, once gone, is gone forever. But I tell you, Ikkyu is right. You can hear ancient music in the pines – I have heard it – but a shift, a total change, a change of gestalt, is needed. Then you can see Buddha preaching again and you can hear Buddha speaking again. You can hear the ancient music in the pines because it is eternal music, it is never lost.

You have lost the capacity to hear it. The music is eternal. Once you regain your capacity, suddenly it is again there. It has always been there, only you were not there. Be herenow, and you can also see clouds a thousand miles away and hear ancient music in the pines.

Change more and more towards the right hemisphere. Become more and more feminine, more and more loving, surrendering, trusting; more and more close to the whole. Don't try to be an island, become part of the continent.

Enough for today.

Chapter 2

The Meaning of Maturity

? You told me that my mind is immature. What does it mean to have a mind that is mature?

To think that you know is to be immature. To function from knowledge, from conclusion, is immaturity. To function from no-knowledge, from no conclusion, from no past, is maturity.

Maturity is deep trust in your own consciousness; immaturity is a distrust in your own consciousness. And when you distrust your consciousness you trust your knowledge, but that is a substitute, and a very poor substitute at that.

Try to understand this, it is important. You have been living, you have experienced so many things; you have read, you have listened, you have thought. Now all those conclusions are there. When a certain situation arises you can function in two ways. Either you can function through all the accumulated past, according to it — that's what I mean by functioning through a center, through conclusions, through experience, stale, dead — then whatsoever you do, your response is not going to be a response, it will be a reaction. And to be reactionary is to be immature.

If you can function right now, here in this moment, through your consciousness, through your being aware, putting aside all that you have known, this is what I call functioning through no-knowledge. This is functioning through innocence. — and this is maturity.

I was reading one anecdote:

It seemed to Mr. Smith that now that his son had turned thirteen, it was important to discuss those matters which an adolescent ought to know about life. So he called the boy into the study one evening. shut the door carefully, and said with impressive dignity, "Son, I would like to discuss the facts of life with you."

"Sure thing, Dad," said the boy. "What do you want to know?"

The mind is immature when it is not ready to learn. The ego feels very fulfilled if you need not learn anything from anybody; the ego feels very enhanced if it feels that it already knows. Now the problem is that life goes on changing, it is never the same — it goes on flowing, it is a flux — and your knowledge is always the same. Your knowledge is not evolving with life, it is stuck somewhere in the past. Whenever you react through it you will miss the point, because it will not be exactly the right thing to do. Life has changed but your knowledge remains the same and you act out of this knowledge. That means you face today with your yesterday's knowledge. You will never be able to be alive. The more you function through knowledge the more immature you become.

Now let me tell you a paradox: every child who is innocent is mature. Maturity has nothing to do with age because it has nothing to do with experience. Maturity has something to do with responsiveness, freshness, virginity, innocence. So when I use the word *mature* I don't mean that when you become more experienced you will be more mature. That's what people usually mean when they use the word. I don't mean that. The more you gather knowledge, the more your mind will become immature. And by the time you are seventy or eighty you will be completely immature because you will have a stale past to function through.

Watch a small child: knowing nothing, having no experience, he functions here and now. That's why children can learn more than aged people. Psychologists say that if a child is not forced to learn, not forced to discipline himself, he can learn any foreign language in three months. Just left to himself with people who know the language, he will catch it in three months. But if you force him to learn it will take almost three years – because the more you force the more he starts functioning through whatsoever he learns, through yesterday's knowledge. If he is left to himself he moves freely, spontaneously; learning comes easily, by itself, of its own accord.

By the time the child reaches the age of eight he has learned almost seventy percent of whatsoever he is going to learn in his whole life. He may live eighty years, but by the time he is eight he has learned seventy percent – he will learn only thirty percent more, and every day his capacity to learn will be less and less and less. The more he knows, the less he learns. When people use the word *maturity* they mean more knowledge; when I use the word *maturity* I mean the capacity to learn – not to know but to learn. And they are different, totally different, diametrically opposite things.

Knowledge is a dead thing. The capacity to learn is an alive process: you simply remain capable of learning, you simply remain available, you simply remain open, ready to receive. Learning is receptivity. Knowledge makes you less receptive because you go on thinking that you already know: what is there to learn? When you already know you miss much, when you don't know anything you cannot miss anything.

In his old age Socrates said, "Now I know nothing!" That was maturity. At the very end he said, "I know nothing."

Life is so vast. How can this tiny mind know? At the most, glimpses are enough; even they are too much. Existence is so tremendously vast and infinite, beginningless, endless – how can this tiny drop of consciousness know it? This is enough, that even a few glimpses come, a few doors open, a few moments happen when you come in contact with existence. But those moments cannot be turned into knowledge. And your mind tends to do it. Then it becomes more and more immature.

So the first thing is that you should be capable of learning and your learning capacity should never be burdened by knowledge, should never be covered by dust. The mirror of learning should remain clean and fresh so it can go on reflecting.

The mind can function in two ways. It can either function like a film in a camera: once exposed, finished, the film immediately becomes knowledgeable and it loses its learning capacity. Exposed once, and it already knows: now it is useless, now it is not capable of learning more. If you expose it again and again it will become more and more confused. That's why people who know too much are always afraid of learning, because they will become confused. They are films that are already exposed.

Then there is another type of learning: learning like a mirror. Expose the mirror for a thousand and one times, it makes no difference: if you come in front of the mirror you are reflected, if you go the reflection goes. The mirror never accumulates. The film in the camera immediately accumulates; it is a miser, it catches hold, clings. But the mirror simply mirrors: you come in front, you are in it, you go, you are gone.

This is the way to remain mature. Every child is born mature and almost all people die immature. This will look very paradoxical, but this is so. Remain innocent and you will remain mature.

The second thing is that the immature mind is always interested in trivia. The immature mind is always interested in things: money, houses, cars, power, prestige – all trivia, all rot. The mature mind is interested only in existence, in being, in life itself. So when I say to you that you have an immature mind I mean you are still interested in things, not in persons, still interested in the outside, not in the inside, still interested in objects, not in subjectivity; still interested in the finite, not interested in the infinite.

Just watch your mind, where it moves, what its fantasies are. If you find a valuable diamond on the road and just there by its side a rose has flowered, in what will you be interested, in the rose or in the diamond? You will not be able to see the rose if you are interested in the diamond. You will simply miss the rose: "It is valueless." Your eyes will be too clouded by the diamond. Your whole mind will become focused on the diamond and you will miss another diamond which was more alive – the rose.

In the Hindu paradise they say roses are not ordinary roses, they are made of diamonds. I don't know, but I have seen roses. If you can see roses here, exactly on this earth – not in paradise but here, now – they are made of diamonds, so why go far away? Once you know how to see a rose there is nothing comparable to it. And once you can see the rose you may forget completely about the diamond.

It happened that Mulla Nasruddin came to me one day. He was very much worried and he said, "Ah, poor Mr. Jones. Did you hear what happened to him? He tripped at the top of the stairs, fell down the whole flight, banged his head and died."

Shocked, I said, "Died?"

"Died," he repeated with emphasis, "and broke his glasses too!"

The immature mind is more interested in glasses than in life and death and love, more interested in things, houses, cars. When I tell you that you have an immature mind, I mean you are still interested in that which is worthless, nonessential. At the most it can be used, at the most it can become a decoration in life, but it cannot replace life, it cannot be a substitute for life, it cannot become life itself. And there are many people who have made it a life.

I know a few rich people who live such beggarly lives, one cannot imagine it ...

I used to know a man in Delhi who had six bungalows, all out on rent, and he lived in a small dark cell with no children and no wife.

I asked him once, "You have enough. Why do you go on living in this small dark cell? Why have you imposed this imprisonment upon yourself? What penance are you doing?"

He said, "None. I have always lived this way and it is perfectly beautiful. And people are living in those six bungalows."

He goes to those bungalows only to collect rent.

I asked him, "Why have you never married?"

"I am a poor man and women are very costly. I could not afford it," he said.

If you meet that man you will not be able to recognize that he owns six big houses and earns a lot of money. What has happened to this man? He is more interested in money than he is in himself; he is more interested in money than he is in love; he is more interested in the power that money brings – but he has never shared anything with anybody.

These people are not rare, they are very common. And everybody has such a tendency inside. And people go on rationalizing. That man is very clever. He says, "This is not miserliness. Please don't misunderstand me. I am a simple man, I live a simple life. I am a religious man, and a simple life is beautiful."

If you are too interested in things, you are immature. Shift your attention. Become more and more interested in people rather than in yourself.

I have a *sannyasin* here. She always falls in love with beggarly people and she is tremendously rich.

Just a few days ago, she came and asked, "Why, Osho, do I go on falling in love with beggarly people, people who are almost on the street?"

I know the reason why: with a beggarly man she need not be worried about her money – and she thinks that she is helping these people with food, with small things. In fact she has never fallen in love. She is so much in love with money that she cannot fall in love with people. In fact she purchases these people for money; they are without any cost, without any risk. And they feel obliged because she gives food and clothing and a shelter; they feel obliged so they pretend that they love her, and she goes on pretending that she has fallen in love. This is a way to protect the money and this is a way to remain closed, miserly.

And she is suffering, in pain, but she cannot see the point. She has to learn how to share. If you know how to share, you are mature. If you don't know how to share, you are immature.

And this sharing goes on, on all levels, in all directions, in all dimensions. Whatsoever you have, you share. And this is one of the most basic things to understand: that the more you share something, the more it grows in you. Share whatsoever you have and it will grow; cling to it, become afraid of sharing, of friendship, of love, and it will shrink. Life knows only one law, and that law is of expansion, of sharing.

Look at nature. Nature is such a spendthrift. When one flower is needed, a thousand and one flowers will bloom. When you make love to a woman or to a man, in each orgasm millions of cells are released. One would have been enough because at the most one child can be conceived, but millions of cells are released. One man can populate the whole earth – just one man! One ordinary man has intercourse at least four thousand times in his life – an ordinary man – and each time millions of cells are released. The whole world, the whole population that exists right now, can be produced by one man. And if in the West, that man will become the father of only two or three, if in the East, twelve, fourteen, fifteen – that's all. For fifteen persons to be conceived, millions of cells are released.

Nature is a spendthrift. Where one flower is needed it produces millions. One tree will produce ... Look at this *gulmohr* – millions of seeds are ready. They will all fall down and a few – one, two, four, five, ten, twenty, a hundred – may become trees. Why so many seeds? Existence is not a miser. If you ask for one it gives millions. Just ask! Jesus has said: "Knock and the doors shall be opened unto you, ask and it shall be given." Remember, if you ask for one, millions will be given.

The moment you become miserly you are closed to the basic phenomenon of life: expansion, sharing. The moment you start clinging to things you have missed the target; you have missed because things are not the target; you, your innermost being, is the target – not a beautiful house but a beautiful you, not a lot of money but a rich you, not many things but an open being available to millions of things.

When I say you are immature I mean you are too concerned with things and you have not yet learned that life consists of consciousness, of beings, not of things. Things are to be used. They are needed, but don't start living by them. Man cannot live by bread alone: once living by bread alone, by things alone, you are already dead.

And the third thing: maturity is always spontaneous; it does not plan, it makes no rehearsals. People come to me ...

Just the other night somebody was here. He said, "I prepare so many questions when I come to see you, but when I come here I forget. What do you do to me?"

I am not doing anything at all! It is you. The moment you prepare something you are already saying that it is false. The real thing need not be prepared. Rehearsals are not needed in life, they are needed in a drama. A drama is a false thing. If you prepare your questions, it means those questions are not yours.

If you are thirsty and you come to me, will you forget that you are thirsty and you would like your thirst to be quenched? How can you forget? In fact, when you come by the side of a river your thirst will burn more intensely because the moment you see the water flowing and hear the sound of gurgling, immediately all that you have been suppressing will bubble up, it will respond. Your whole being will say, "I am thirsty!" If you are thirsty you will not forget.

But you prepare questions. You prepare yourself to go to the river and say, "I am very thirsty." What is the point of preparing? If you are thirsty, you are. If you are not thirsty, by the time you reach to the river you will forget about it.

When I say you are immature I mean that you prepare your questions, your inquiries. They are mind things, they don't come from your heart. They are not related to you, they have no roots in you.

It is related in George Bernard Shaw's life that once, at the opening of one of his plays, he stepped forward at its conclusion with obvious complaisance, to accept the rousing plaudits of the crowd.

There was one dissenter, however, who seized the occasion of a lull in the applause to call out in stentorian tones, "Shaw, your play stinks!"

There was a momentary horrified silence, but Shaw, unperturbed, exclaimed from the stage, "My friend, I agree with you completely, but what are we two ... " here he waved his hand over the audience " ... against the great majority?"

And applause returned more loudly than ever.

You cannot prepare something like that. It is impossible. It is a spontaneous response, hence the beauty of it. You cannot prepare for such things. And life is such a continuous thing: either you act immediately or you miss. Later on you will find a thousand and one answers – you could have said this, you could have said that – but they are of no use.

Mark Twain was coming back home with his wife from a lecture hall where he had just delivered a beautiful talk. His wife had not been present, she had just come to pick him up.

On the way she asked, "How was the lecture?"

Mark Twain said, "Which one? The one that I prepared, the one that I delivered, or the one that I am thinking now that I should have delivered? Which one?"

If you prepare, this is going to be so. Remain conscious, alert, aware, and act out of your spontaneity. And not only will others see the alive response of it, you also will be thrilled by your own response. Not only will others be surprised, you will also be surprised yourself.

I call a mind mature which retains the capacity to be surprised. A mind is mature if it goes on continuously being surprised by others, by himself, by everything. Life is a constant wonder: he has no readymade plans for it, no readymade responses for it. He never knows what is going to happen, he moves into the unknown each moment. He never jumps ahead of himself, he never lags behind himself. He remains simply himself, wherever he is.

And, the last and most basic thing: when I say that you have an immature mind, basically I mean that you have a mind. Mind as such is immature. Only no-mind is mature.

Maturity has nothing to do with mind because mind means all that you know. Mind means your experiences, mind means your past, your rehearsals, your preparations. All these things are implied in the word *mind*. Mind is not something in particular, it is the whole accumulation, all the junk, the whole heap of your dead past.

When I say, "Be mature," I mean become a no-mind. If you act spontaneously you will act out of no-mind. If you remain capable of learning you will remain capable of being a no-mind again and again and again; the mind will never be accumulated. If you are capable of remaining alert and spontaneous, able to be surprised by life and by yourself, by and by you will become more and more interested in the interiormost life, in the very core of life. When you see a person you will not see just the body; your gaze will become penetrating, your gaze will become like an X-ray. It will catch hold of the person, of the consciousness there, of the inner light there in the other person. The body is just an abode: you will meet the person, you will shake hands, but not only hands – you will shake the person, you will meet the person.

And in your own life, by and by, you will become aware that the body is just the outermost garment: you have to take care of it, it is not to be neglected, it is valuable, but it is not the end. And you are the master, not the servant. By and by, the more you penetrate withinwards, you will see the mind also is an innermost garment, more valuable than the body but not more valuable than you. *You* remain the supreme value.

And once you know your supreme value, you have become mature. And once you know your supreme value, you know the supreme value of all. All beings are buddhas. Nobody is less than that; and the whole of life is divine. You are always walking on holy ground.

It is said that when Moses went to the hill to meet his God, the bush was afire and from behind the bush he heard, "Stop! Take your shoes off. This is holy ground." I have always liked it, loved it. But all ground is holy ground and all bushes are afire with godliness. If you have not seen this yet you have missed much. Look again: all bushes are afire with godliness and from every bush comes the commandment, "Stop and take your shoes off. This is holy ground you are walking on."

All ground, the whole earth, the whole existence is sacred. Once you have that feeling entering you, I will call you mature, not before that. A mature mind is a religious mind.

❓ Why do I make mountains out of molehills?

Because the ego does not feel good, at ease, with molehills, it wants mountains. Even if it is a misery it should not be a molehill, it should be an Everest. Even if it is misery the ego doesn't want to be ordinarily miserable, it wants to be extraordinarily miserable!

Bernard Shaw is reported to have said, "If I am not going to be the first in heaven, I would like to go to hell – but I would like to be the first."

In Christianity there is only one hell and Bernard Shaw never knew that in India we have a concept of seven hells. If he had heard about Hindu hells he would have chosen the seventh, because in the fifth he would have felt humiliated: others are still far ahead of him, in the seventh. The real sinners, the great sinners, are in the seventh! Either this way or that, but one wants to be the first. Hence one goes on making mountains out of molehills.

A woman hypochondriac died. The whole town felt relieved, the whole medical profession felt relieved, because she was a constant trouble to many people's heads, everywhere, all around. The family, the doctors, the physicians

– she had troubled everybody and nobody was of any help. And she relished the idea that nobody knew anything about the sort of disease she was suffering from – it was an extraordinary disease. In fact there was no disease.

Then she died, and it was almost a celebration in the town. But when they opened her will, she had written in her will that her request had positively to be fulfilled. Her request was that a carved tombstone had to be put on her tomb with these words inscribed on it: "Now will you believe I was sick?"

In this way she would haunt the whole town again.

People go on and on, creating big problems out of nothing. I have talked to thousands of people about their problems and I have not come across a real problem yet. All problems are bogus. You create them because without problems you feel empty. Then there is nothing to do, nothing to fight with, nowhere to go.

People go from one guru to another, from one master to another, from one psychoanalyst to another, from one encounter group to another, because if they don't go they feel empty and they suddenly feel life to be meaningless. You create problems so that you can feel that life is a great work, a growth, and you have to struggle hard.

The ego can exist only when it struggles, remember, when it fights. And if I tell you, "Kill three flies and you will become enlightened," you will not believe me. You will say, "Three flies? There doesn't seem to be much to that. And I will become enlightened? That doesn't seem to be likely." If I say you will have to kill seven hundred lions, of course that looks more like it!

The greater the problem the greater the challenge – and with challenge your ego arises, soars high. You create problems, problems don't exist.

And now if you allow me, there are not even molehills. That too is your trick. You say, "Yes, there may not be mountains, but molehills … ?" No, not even molehills are there, those are your creations. First you create molehills out of nothing, then you create mountains out of molehills. And the priests and the psychoanalysts and the gurus are happy because their whole trade exists because of you. If you don't create molehills out of nothing and you don't make your molehills into mountains, what will be the point of gurus helping you? First you have to be in a shape to be helped.

The real masters have been saying something else. They have been saying: "Please look at what you are doing, what nonsense you are doing. First you create a problem and then you go in search of a solution. Just watch why you are creating the problem. Just exactly in the beginning, when you are creating the problem, is the solution: don't create it!" But that won't appeal to you because then you are suddenly thrown flat upon yourself. Nothing to do? No enlightenment? No satori? No *samadhi*? And you are deeply restless, empty, trying to stuff yourself with anything whatsoever.

You don't have any problems. Only this much has to be understood. This very moment you can drop all problems because they are your creations. Have another look at your problems, and the deeper you look, the smaller they will appear. Go on looking at them and by and by they will start disappearing. Go on gazing and suddenly you will find there is emptiness – a beautiful emptiness surrounds you. Nothing to do, nothing to be, because you are already that.

Enlightenment is not something to be achieved, it is just to be lived. When I say that I achieved enlightenment, I simply mean one day I decided to live it: enough is enough! And since then I have lived it. It is a decision that now you are not interested in creating problems, that's all. It is a decision that now you are finished with all this nonsense of creating problems and finding solutions.

It is a game you are playing with yourself: you yourself are hiding and you yourself are seeking. You are both parties – and you know it! That's why when I say it you smile, you laugh. I am not talking about anything ridiculous; you understand it. You are laughing at yourself. Just watch yourself laughing, just look at your own smile. You understand it. It has to be so because it is your own game: you are hiding and waiting for yourself to be able to seek and find yourself. You can find yourself right now because it is you that is hiding.

That's why Zen masters go on hitting. Whenever somebody comes and says, "I would like to be a buddha," the master gets very angry, because he is asking nonsense – he *is* a buddha. If Buddha comes to me and asks how to be a buddha, what am I supposed to do? I will hit his head: "Who do you think you are befooling? You are a buddha."

Don't make unnecessary trouble for yourself. And understanding will dawn on you if you watch how you make a problem bigger and bigger and bigger, how you spin it, and how you help the wheel to move faster and faster and faster. Then suddenly you are at the top of your misery and you are in need of the whole world's sympathy.

One sannyasin, Marga, wrote me a letter. She said, "Osho, I feel very sad because when you talk, you look at everyone except me." Now, I am not looking at anybody, but I have got eyes so they have to be somewhere. It is not that I am looking at somebody; I am not looking at anybody. And you can see in my eyes that they are empty, they are vacant. But if you are trying to find your reflection in them and you don't, great sadness comes to you.

Now there is a new problem, now the ego feels hurt. Looking at everybody else except you! Just watch how you have made yourself an exception; you have become extraordinary: I look at everybody, the ordinary mass, except you. You have become unique. If I look at Marga – which I am not going to do; since I received her letter I am never going to look at her – if I look at her then the ego can have another trip: that I look only at her. Then that will create a problem!

You are a great problem creator. Just understand this, and suddenly problems disappear. You are perfectly in shape. You are born perfect – that is the whole message. You are born perfect, perfection is your innermost nature. You have just to live it. Decide, and live it.

If you are not yet fed up with the game, you can continue, but don't ask why – you know. The "why" is simple: the ego cannot exist in emptiness, it needs something to fight with. Even a ghost of your imagination will do, but you need to fight with someone. The ego exists only in conflict. The ego is not an entity, it is a tension. Whenever there is a conflict the tension arises and the ego exists; when there is no conflict the tension disappears and the ego disappears. Ego is not a thing, it is just a tension.

And of course nobody wants small tensions, everybody wants big tensions. If your own problems are not enough you start thinking about humanity and the world and the future; socialism, communism, and all that rubbish. You start thinking about it as if the whole world depends on your advice. Then you think, "What is going to happen in Israel? What is going to happen in Africa?" And you go on advising, and you create problems.

People become very excited, they cannot sleep because there is some war going on. They become very excited. Their own life is so ordinary that they will have to reach extraordinariness from some other source. The nation is in diffi-culty so they become identified with the nation. The culture is in difficulty, the society is in difficulty – now there are big problems and you become identified. You are a Hindu and the Hindu culture is in difficulty; you are a Christian and the church is in difficulty. The whole world is at stake – now you become big through your problem.

The ego needs some problems. If you understand this, in the very under-standing, the mountains become molehills again and then the molehills also disappear. Suddenly there is emptiness, pure emptiness all around. This is what enlightenment is all about: a deep understanding that there is no problem.

Then, with no problem to solve, what will you do? Immediately you will start living. You will eat, you will sleep, you will love, you will have a chit-chat, you will sing, you will dance – what else is there to do? You have become a god, you have started living.

If there is any God, one thing is certain: he must not be having any problems. That much is certain. Then what is he doing with all his time? No problems, no psychiatrist to consult, no gurus to go and surrender to. What is God doing? He must be getting crazy, whirling. What will he do? No, he is living; his life is totally full with life. He must be eating, sleeping, dancing, having a love affair – but without any problems.

Start living this moment and you will see that the more you live, the fewer problems there are, because now that your emptiness is flowering in living, there is no need. When you don't live, the same energy goes sour. The same energy which would have become a flower, is stuck. Not being allowed to bloom it becomes a thorn in the heart; it is the same energy.

Force a small child to sit in the corner and tell him to become completely immobile, unmoving. Watch what happens. Just a few minutes earlier he was perfectly at ease, flowing; now his face will become red because he will have to strain, hold himself. His whole body will become rigid; he will try to fidget here and there and he will want to jump out of himself. You have forced the energy: now it has no purpose, no meaning, no space to move, nowhere to bloom and flower; it is stuck, frozen, rigid. The child is suffering a short death, a temporary death. Now if you don't allow the child to run again and move around the garden and play, he will start creating problems. He will fantasize: in his mind he will create problems and start fighting with those problems. He will see a big dog and he will get afraid, or he will see a ghost and he will have to fight and escape from him. Now he is creating problems. The same energy that just a few minutes before was flowing all around, in all directions, is stuck and becoming sour.

If people can dance a little more, sing a little more, be a little more crazy, their energy will be more flowing and their problems will, by and by, disappear. Hence I insist so much on dance. Dance to orgasm! Let the whole energy become dance, and suddenly you will see that you don't have any head: the stuck energy in the head is moving all around, creating beautiful patterns, gestures, movement. And when you dance there comes a moment when your body is no longer a rigid thing; it becomes flexible, flowing. When you dance there comes a moment when your boundary is no longer so clear; you melt and merge with the cosmos, the boundaries are mixing.

Watch a dancer: you will see that he has become an energy phenomenon, no longer in a fixed form, no longer in a frame. He is flowing out of his frame, out of his form and becoming more alive, more and more alive. But only if you dance yourself will you know what really happens: the head inside disappears, again you are a child. Then you don't create any problems.

Live, dance, eat, sleep – do things as totally as possible. And remember again and again: whenever you catch yourself creating any problem, slip out of it, immediately. Once you get into the problem then a solution will be needed. And even if you find a solution, out of that solution a thousand and one problems will arise again. Once you miss the first step you are in the trap. Whenever you see that now you are slipping into a problem, catch hold of yourself, run, jump, dance, but don't get into the problem. Do something immediately so that the energy that was creating the problem becomes fluid, unfrozen, melts, goes back to the cosmos.

Primitive people don't have many problems. I have come across primitive groups in India who say they don't dream at all. Freud would not be able to believe that it is possible. They don't dream, and if sometimes somebody dreams – it is a rare phenomenon – the whole village fasts, prays to God. Something has gone wrong, something wrong has happened – a man has dreamed.

It never happens in their tribe because they live so totally that nothing is left in the head to be completed in sleep. Whatsoever you leave incomplete has to be completed in your dreams; whatsoever you have not lived remains as a hangover and completes itself in the mind. That's what a dream is.

The whole day you go on thinking. The thinking simply shows that you have more energy than you use for living, you have more energy than your so-called life needs. You are missing real life. Use more energy, then fresh energies will be flowing. Just don't be a miser. Use them today, let today be complete unto itself; tomorrow will take care of itself, don't be worried about tomorrow. The worry, the problem, the anxiety, all simply show one thing: that you are not living rightly, that your life is not yet a celebration, a dance, a festivity – hence all the problems.

If you live, ego disappears. Life knows no ego, it knows only living and living and living. Life knows no self, no center; life knows no separation. You breathe, life enters into you; you exhale, you enter into life. There is no separation. You eat and trees enter into you through the fruit. Then one day you die, you are buried in the earth, and the trees suck you up and you become fruits. Your children will eat you again. You have been eating your ancestors; the trees have converted them into fruits. You think you are a vegetarian? Don't be deceived by appearances – we are all cannibals!

Life is one. It goes on moving, it comes into you, it passes through you. In fact to say that it comes into you is not right, because it seems as if life comes into you and then passes out of you. You don't exist, only this life's coming and going. You don't exist, only life exists in its tremendous forms, in its energy, in its millions of delights. Once you understand this, let that understanding be the only law.

Start living as buddhas from this moment. If you decide otherwise, it is for you to decide. But as I see it, it is a decision: "I am not going to befool myself anymore. Now I start living as a Buddha, in emptiness. I will not try to find unnecessary occupation. I dissolve."

? **I notice that deep down I want to be loved, accepted, like the greatest man on earth, that I want to be the most famous person. And I feel hurt when someone rejects me. What to do with these dreams?**

If you understand that they are dreams then wash your face and have a cup of tea. What is there to be done about it? Dreams are dreams, why be bothered? But you don't understand that they are dreams.

This is borrowed. You know that they are not dreams, that's why you are worried. Otherwise why be worried? If in a dream you see that you have fallen ill, when you wake up in the morning do you go to the doctor? "In my dream I was very ill and now some medication is needed"? You never go. By the morning you realize it was a dream, finished! What is the point of going to a doctor?

But you have not yet understood that these are dreams. These are realities for you, hence the problem.

"I notice that deep down I want to be loved." If you want to be loved, love! – because whatsoever you give is returned. If you want to be loved forget about wanting to be loved. Love, and in a thousand ways love will come to you. Life reflects, life resounds, life echoes whatsoever you throw at life. So if you want to be loved forget about wanting and being loved, that is not the point at all then. Then the rule is simple: love.

And if you want to be accepted like the greatest man on earth, then start accepting everybody as the greatest man on earth otherwise how are they going to accept you as the greatest? They are also on the same trip. They are not going to accept you as the greatest because then what will happen to them? If you are the greatest, then who are they? Nobody wants to be anything else.

Once it happened, a friend of Mulla Nasruddin was talking to Mulla. They met after many years. Both were bitter rivals, both were poets. Both started to boast about the progress they had made in their careers.

"You have no idea, Nasruddin, how many people read my poetry now," bragged his friend. "My readers have doubled."

"My God, my God!" cried Nasruddin. "I had no idea you had got married!"

Everybody is on the same trip. If you want people to accept you as the greatest man on earth, let this be the rule: whatsoever you want others to do for you, do for them. But that is the trouble. The ego wants you to be the greatest man on earth and nobody else. Then you will feel hurt because all are on the same trip.

Can't you understand the simple point? They are also waiting for you to accept them as the greatest man.

I heard Mulla Nasruddin once. He was delivering a political speech.

He said, "It is with some trepidation that I address an audience of people all of whom are smarter than I am – all of them put together, that is."

Everybody is trying to be at the top of the world; then you are in competition with the whole world. Remember, you are going to be defeated. One man fighting against the whole world – that is the situation.

If you see the point, there are two ways. Either forget about this trip, be ordinary, simple, whatsoever you are. There is no need to be great, the only need is to be real. Greatness is the wrong goal. To be real ...

I have come across a hip slogan: "Be realistic, plan for a miracle" Yes, that is how it is. If you are really realistic, you start living the miracle. And the miracle is, if you are real you don't want to be bothered with competition, comparison. Who bothers? You enjoy your food, you enjoy your breathing, you enjoy the sunlight, you enjoy the stars, you enjoy life, you enjoy being alive – you are perfectly in tune, in harmony with the whole. What is the point of being a great man? The great men, the so-called great men, are almost always phony. They have to be, they cannot be real persons. They are plastic because they have chosen a wrong goal. To be great is an ego goal, to be real is existential.

If you want to be great you will be in continuous conflict. And of course you will be hurt by everybody. Not that everybody is trying to hurt you, but they are doing their trip and you are unnecessarily coming in their way.

Get out of this rat race. Sit under the tree by the side of the road. It is tremendously beautiful and silent. Otherwise, be ready to be hurt.

A politician used to come to me. Once he was the president of the Indian National Congress, a great man in India.

He told me, "I am such a simple man. Why do people go on spreading nasty things about me? Why do people want to hurt me?"

I told him, "Nobody wants to hurt you. You are unnecessarily coming in their way. They also want to be presidents of great parties – you are standing in their way. They have to push you away." I told him, "Just remember what you did to the president before you. They are trying to do the same thing with you – leg-pulling."

Once you are in a power post, you are continuously being pulled and pushed. It has to be so.

Ramakrishna used to tell a beautiful story:

A bird was flying with a dead mouse and twenty or thirty birds were chasing him. The bird was very worried.

"Why? I am not doing anything to them, I am just carrying my dead mouse. Why are they all after me?"

And they hit him hard and in the conflict, in the struggle, the bird opened his mouth and dropped the mouse. Immediately they all flew towards the mouse, they all forgot about him.

Then he sat upon a tree and brooded.

They were not against him. They were also on the same trip – they wanted the mouse.

If people are hurting you, open your mouth. You must be carrying a dead mouse! Drop it! And then sit, if you can, sit on the tree or under the tree and brood. And suddenly you will see that they have forgotten about you. They are not concerned. They never were concerned. The ego is a dead mouse.

Jones' oldest daughter had just given birth to a beautiful baby and Jones was being congratulated.

He looked downcast, however, and a friend said, "What's the matter, Jones? Don't you like the idea of being a grandfather?"

Jones heaved an enormous sigh. "No," he said, "I don't, but that doesn't bother me so much. It is just that it is so humiliating to have to go to bed with a grandmother."

Just watch your mind, how it creates problems. The woman remains the same but now she has become a grandmother, and one feels humiliated.

It is your idea that is giving you humiliation. If you are really concerned with your own wellbeing then nobody is hurting you – just your own ideas. Drop them.

Or, if you feel good with them, don't be worried about the hurts. Then carry them. But have a decision inside: if you want the ego trip, if you want to be the greatest man in the world, then everybody is going to prove that you are the worst man in the world. Then have courage and heart to suffer all that. It is futile, but if you choose that way, it is your choice. If you really want your wellbeing and your inner calm and silence and bliss, then these hurts are indicative: you are carrying some wrong ideas within you. Drop those ideas.

? **I don't have a question – just a feeling of hopelessness. I can't believe my questions, I have a feeling they come from something brittle and unreal.**

"I don't have a question – just a feeling of hopelessness." How does hopelessness arise? You must be hoping too much. It comes out of too much hope.

If you don't hope, all hopelessness disappears. If you expect too much, frustration is bound to come. If you are trying to succeed, you will fail. Whatsoever you want to try too hard, just the opposite will happen.

You must have been trying too hard to fulfill some hope – then hopelessness comes. If you really want to get rid of hopelessness – and everybody wants that – then get rid of hope. Drop all hope, and suddenly you will see that with the hope, hopelessness has disappeared. Then one comes to an inner tranquility where no hope exists, and no hopelessness. One is simply calm and quiet and collected – a deep reservoir of energy, a pool of energy, cool.

But for that you have to sacrifice hope. The very question shows that you are still hoping. Go a little deeper and further: if you are really hopeless, hopelessness will disappear.

Let me tell it to you another way. Whenever a person says that he is hopeless he simply says he is still clinging to the same hope which has proved to be futile, of which there is no indication of being fulfilled at all. But still one goes on holding it, hoping against all hope. Then hopelessness continues.

Don't hope for anything. There is no need because all that you can hope for is already given. What more can you hope for?

You are here, everything is here, just being is all. But you don't appreciate, you are asking for some dead mouse, some power trip, some ego trip, some success in the eyes of the world. Those are not going to be fulfilled. Even Alexanders have failed. Even Alexander dies a poor man, a beggar, because everything that you accumulate is snatched back from you, you go empty-handed. Empty-handed you come, empty-handed you go.

So why bother about success, riches, power – material or spiritual? Just be. And being is the greatest miracle. Just turn within yourself, what Buddha calls *paravritti*. Turn yourself – a complete turn, a total turn – and suddenly you are so full of joy you don't need anything. In fact you have so much that you would like to shower it on others.

But things go on moving from one extreme to another. If you hope, by and by the pendulum moves towards hopelessness. If you are too much in love with life, by and by you move towards suicide. If you are too religious, by and by you move and become anti-religious. The pendulum goes on moving towards the opposite. Somewhere in the middle, one has to stop.

And if you stop in the middle, time stops with you. And when time stops, all hope, all desires have stopped. You start living right now. Now is the only time and here is the only space.

Let me tell you one story. It is a very beautiful Jewish anecdote.

Young Sammy Moskowitz had just bought himself a motor scooter, but he had been brought up in very orthodox fashion and wasn't the least bit sure whether it was fitting for an orthodox Jew to ride one. He thought that the best way out would be to go to his reverend rabbi to teach him a *barucha*, a traditional prayer of blessing, to intone over the motor scooter before he drove it. Surely that would make it proper for him to use it?

He therefore approached his rabbi and said, "Rabbi, I have bought a motor scooter and I wish to know if you could teach me a *barucha* to say over it each morning."

The rabbi said, "What is a motor scooter?"

Sammy explained, and the rabbi shook his head. "As far as I know, there is no appropriate *barucha* for the occasion and I strongly suspect that riding a motor scooter is a sin. I forbid you to use it."

Sammy was very downhearted, for from his very soul he longed to drive his motor scooter, which had set him back a considerable sum. A thought occurred to him: why not seek a second and perhaps more liberal opinion from a rabbi who was not orthodox, but merely conservative?

He found a conservative rabbi who unlike the orthodox rabbi earlier consulted, was not in the traditional long coat at all but wore a dark business suit. The conservative rabbi said, "What is a motor scooter?"

Sammy explained. The rabbi thought for a while, then said, "I suppose there's nothing wrong about riding a motor scooter. But still I don't know of any appropriate *barucha*, and if your conscience hurts you without one, then don't drive it."

He journeyed out to the suburbs and met Rabbi Richmond Ellis, in his knickerbockers, about to leave for the golf links on his motor scooter.

Sammy grew terribly excited, "It's all right for a Jew to ride a motor scooter?" he said. "I've got one but I didn't know."

"Sure, kid," said the rabbi. "Nothing wrong with the motor scooter at all. Ride it in good health."

"Then give me a *barucha* for it."

The reformed rabbi thought, then said, "What is a *barucha*?"

Things move from one extreme to another! The orthodox rabbi doesn't know what a motor scooter is, and the progressive one is not aware of what a *barucha* is. From religion, too much dogmatic religion, people become too irreligious. When they leave the church they move to the prostitute.

Somewhere a deep balance is needed. Just between the two, exactly between the two, is transcendence.

So you have lived with hope. Now the hope has failed and you are living in hopelessness. Now let hopelessness also fail: drop hope and hopelessness together. Just transcend that attitude which lives in the future. Live herenow! Living in hope is living in the future, which is really postponing life. It is not a way of living but a way of suicide. There is no need for any hope and there is no need to feel hopeless. Live herenow. Life is tremendously blissful, it is showering here and you are looking somewhere else. It is just in front of your eyes but your eyes have moved far away, they look at the horizon. It is within you but you are not there.

I am not for hope, I am not for hopelessness. I am against all extremism. All excess is futile.

Buddha used to say, "My path is the middle path – *majjhim nikaya.*" That is the path of transcendence.

Enough for today.

Chapter 3

The Halo of Yakushi-Buddha

*One winter day, a masterless samurai came to Eisai's temple and
made an appeal: I'm poor and sick," he said, "and my family is
dying of hunger. Please help us, master."*

*Dependent as he was on widows' mites, Eisai's life was very austere,
and he had nothing to give. He was about to send the samurai off
when he remembered the image of Yakushi-Buddha in the hall.
Going up to it he tore off its halo and gave it to the samurai. "Sell
this," said Eisai, "it should tide you over."*

The bewildered but desperate samurai took the halo and left.

*"Master!" cried one of Eisai's disciples, "that's sacrilege! How could
you do such a thing?"*

*"Sacrilege? Bah! I have merely put the Buddha's mind, which is
full of love and mercy, to use, so to speak. Indeed, if he himself had
heard that poor samurai, he would have cut off a limb for him."*

Meditation is a flower, and compassion is its fragrance. Exactly like
that it happens: the flower blooms and the fragrance spreads on the
winds in all directions, to be carried to the very ends of the earth. But
the basic thing is the blooming of the flower.

Man is also carrying a potential for flowering within him. Until and unless
the inner being of man flowers, the fragrance of compassion is not possible.
Compassion cannot be practiced, it is not a discipline. You cannot manage it,
it is beyond you. If you meditate, one day you suddenly become aware of a
new phenomenon, absolutely strange: compassion is flowing from your being
towards the whole of existence. Undirected, unaddressed, it is moving to the
very ends of existence.

Without meditation, the same energy remains passion; with meditation,
the same energy becomes compassion. Passion and compassion are not two
energies, they are one and the same energy. Once it passes through meditation
it is transformed, transfigured; it becomes qualitatively different. Passion
moves downwards, compassion moves upwards. Passion moves through desire,
compassion moves through desirelessness. Passion is an occupation to forget the
miseries in which you live, compassion is a celebration. Compassion is a dance of
attainment, of fulfillment: you are so fulfilled that you can share. Now there is
nothing left; you have attained the destiny that you were carrying for millennia

within you like an unflowered potentiality, just a bud. Now it has flowered and it is dancing. You have attained, you are fulfilled. There is no more to attain, nowhere to go, nothing to do.

Now what will happen to the energy? You start sharing. The same energy that was moving through the dark layers of passion now moves with light rays upwards, uncontaminated by any desire, uncontaminated by any conditioning, pure, uncorrupted by any motivation; hence I call it *fragrance*. The flower is limited, but not the fragrance. The flower has limitations, it is rooted somewhere, in bondage. But fragrance has no bondage – it simply moves, rides on the winds with no moorings in the earth.

Meditation is a flower, it has roots. It exists in you. Once compassion happens, it is not rooted, it simply moves and goes on moving. Buddha has disappeared, but not his compassion. The flower will die sooner or later; it is part of earth and the dust will return unto dust, but the fragrance that has been released will remain forever and forever. Buddha is gone, Jesus is gone, but not their fragrance. Their compassion still continues, and whoever is open to their compassion will immediately feel its impact, will be moved by it, will be taken on a new journey, on a new pilgrimage.

Compassion is not limited to the flower; it comes from the flower but it is not of the flower. It comes through the flower, the flower is just a passage, but it comes really from the beyond. It cannot come without the flower, the flower is a necessary stage, but it does not belong to the flower. Once the flower has bloomed compassion is released.

This insistence, this emphasis, has to be deeply understood, because if you miss the point you can start practicing compassion, but then it is not a real fragrance. Practiced compassion is just the same passion with a new name. It is the same desire-contaminated, motivation-corrupted energy, and it can become very dangerous to other people – because in the name of compassion you can destroy, in the name of compassion you can make prisoners of other people, in the name of compassion you can create bondage. It is not compassion, and if you practice it you are being artificial, formal, in fact, a hypocrite.

The first thing to be remembered continuously is that compassion cannot be practiced. It is this point where all the followers of all the great religious teachers have missed. Buddha attained compassion through meditation; now Buddhists go on practicing compassion. Jesus attained compassion through meditation but Christians, the Christian missionaries, go on practicing love, compassion, service to humanity. But their compassion has proved to be a very destructive force in the world; their compassion has created only wars, their compassion has destroyed millions of people. They end up in deep imprisonments.

Compassion frees you, gives you freedom; but that compassion has to come only through meditation, there is no other way to it. Buddha has said that compassion is a byproduct, a consequence. You cannot catch hold of the consequence directly, you have to move; you have to produce the cause and the effect follows. So if you really want to understand what compassion is you have to understand what meditation is. Forget all about compassion, it comes of its own accord.

Try to understand what meditation is. Compassion can become a criterion as to whether the meditation was right or not. If the meditation has been right, compassion is bound to come – it is natural, it follows like a shadow. If the meditation has been wrong then compassion will not follow. So compassion can work as a criterion as to whether the meditation has been really right or not.

Even a meditation can be wrong. People have a wrong notion that all meditations are right. It is not so. Meditations can be wrong. For example, any meditation that leads you deep into concentration is wrong, it will not result in compassion. You will become more and more closed rather than becoming open. If you narrow down your consciousness, if you concentrate on something and you exclude the whole of existence and become one-pointed, it will create more and more tension in you. Hence the word *attention*: it means a tension. Concentration, the very sound of the word, gives you a feeling of tenseness.

Concentration has its uses, but it is not meditation. In scientific work, in scientific research, in the science lab, you need concentration. You have to concentrate on one problem and exclude everything else – so much so that you almost become unmindful of the remaining world. The only problem that you are concentrating upon is your world. That's why scientists become absent-minded. People who concentrate too much always become absentminded because they don't know how to remain open to the whole world.

I was reading an anecdote:

"I have brought a frog," said a scientist, a professor of zoology, beaming at his class, "fresh from the pond, in order that we might study its outer appearance and later dissect it."

He carefully unwrapped the package he carried and inside was a neatly prepared ham sandwich. The good professor looked at it with astonishment.

"Odd!" he said, "I distinctly remember having eaten my lunch."

That goes on happening to scientists: they become one-pointed and their whole mind becomes narrow. Of course, a narrow mind has its use: it becomes more penetrating, it becomes like a sharp needle, it hits exactly the right point – but it misses the great life that surrounds you.

A buddha is not a man of concentration, he is a man of awareness. He has not been trying to narrow down his consciousness, on the contrary, he has been trying to drop all barriers so that he becomes totally available to existence. Watch: existence is simultaneous. I am speaking here and the traffic noise is simultaneous, the train, the birds the wind blowing through the trees; in this moment, the whole of existence converges. You listening to me, I speaking to you, and millions of things going on – it is tremendously rich.

Concentration makes you one-pointed at a very great cost: ninety-nine percent of life is discarded. If you are solving a mathematical problem, you cannot listen to the birds, they will be a distraction. Children playing around, dogs barking in the street, they will be a distraction. The wife working in the kitchen washing the plates will be a distraction. Because of concentration people have tried to escape from life, to go to the Himalayas, to go to a cave, to remain isolated, so that you can concentrate on God. But God is not an object. God is this wholeness of existence, this moment; God is the totality. That's why science will never be able to know God.

The very method of science is concentration and because of that method, science can never know God. It can know more and more minute details. First the molecule was thought to be the last particle, then it was divided. Then an even tinier part, the atom, was known, then concentration divided that also. Now there are electrons, protons, neutrons; sooner or later they are also going to be divided.

Science goes on from the smaller to the smaller, and the bigger, the vast, is completely forgotten. The whole is completely forgotten for the part. Because of concentration, science can never know God. So when people come to me and they say, "Osho, teach us concentration, we want to know God," I am simply puzzled. They have not understood the basics of the search.

Science is one-pointed, the search is objective. Religion is simultaneity, the object is the whole, the total. To know the total, that is, to know God, you will have to have a consciousness which is open from everywhere, not confined, not standing in a window. Otherwise the frame of the window will become the frame of existence. Just standing under the sun in the open sky – that is what meditation is. Meditation has no frame: it is not a window, it is not a door. Meditation is not concentration, it is not attention. Meditation is awareness.

So what to do? Repeating a mantra, doing Transcendental Meditation, is not going to help. Transcendental Meditation has become very, very important in America because of the objective approach, because of the scientific mind. Now that is the only meditation on which scientific research work is being done because that is the only meditation on which scientific work *can* be done. It is exactly concentration and not meditation. It is comprehensible for the scientific mind.

In the universities, in the science laboratories, in psychological research work, much is being done about TM because it is not meditation. It is a concentration, a method of concentration; it falls under the same category as scientific concentration. There is a link between the two but it has nothing to do with meditation. Meditation is so vast, so tremendously infinite; no scientific research is possible. Only compassion will show whether the man has achieved or not. Alpha waves won't be of much help because they are still of the mind and meditation is not of the mind, it is something beyond.

So let me tell you a few basic things. One, meditation is not concentration but relaxation. One simply relaxes. One simply relaxes into oneself. The more you relax, the more you feel yourself open, vulnerable. The more you relax, the less rigid you are; you become more flexible and suddenly existence starts penetrating you. You are no longer like a rock, you have openings. Relaxation means allowing yourself to fall into a state where you are not doing anything, because if you are doing something, tension will continue. It is a state of non-doing: you simply relax and you enjoy the feeling of relaxation.

Relax into yourself. Just close your eyes and listen to all that is happening all around — no need to feel anything as a distraction. The moment you feel it is a distraction, you are denying godliness, existence. This moment existence has come to you as a bird — don't deny. It has knocked at your door as a bird. The next moment it has come as a dog, barking, or as a child crying and weeping, or as a madman laughing. Don't deny, don't reject, accept — because if you deny you will become tense. All denials create tension. Accept. If you want to relax, acceptance is the way. Accept whatsoever is happening all around, let it become an organic whole. It is! You may know it, you may not know it, but everything is interrelated. These birds, these trees, this sky, this sun, this earth, you, me, all are related. It is an organic unity. If the sun disappears the trees will disappear, if the trees disappear the birds will disappear, if the birds and trees disappear you cannot be here, you will disappear. It is an ecology; everything is deeply related with everything else.

So don't deny anything, because the moment you deny, you are denying something in you. If you deny these singing birds then something in you is denied.

Once it happened that it was spring. The weather was delightful and I was sitting on a park bench. I was enjoying the spring, the birds, the air and the sun. I was listening to the melodious chirping of numerous birds.

A stranger was also sitting on the same bench. I turned to him and said to him, "Is not the music of the birds delightful?"

But he must have been a religious man: he was doing some mantra. He felt disturbed. He felt as if I had interfered.

He scowled and said, "How the devil can I hear what you are saying over the damned noise of those stupid birds?"

But if you deny, reject; if you feel distracted, if you feel angry, you are rejecting something within you. Just listen again to the birds without any feeling of distraction, anger, and suddenly you will see that the bird within you responds. Then those birds are not there as strangers, intruders. Suddenly, the whole existence becomes a family. It is. And I call a man religious who has come to understand that the whole existence is a family. He may not go to any church and he may not worship in any temple and he may not pray at any mosque or *gurudwara* – that doesn't matter, that is almost irrelevant. If you do, good, it is okay; if you don't that is even better. But one who has understood the organic unity of existence is constantly in the temple, is constantly facing the sacred and the divine.

But if you are doing some stupid mantra you will think these birds are stupid. If you are repeating some nonsense within you or thinking some trivia – you may call it philosophy, religion – then these birds become distractions. Their sounds are simply divine. They don't say anything, they are simply bubbling with delight. Their song has no meaning except an overflowing of energy. They want to share with existence – with the trees, with the flowers, with you. They have nothing to say, they are just being there, themselves.

If you relax, you accept. Acceptance of existence is the only way to relax. If small things disturb you then it is your attitude that is disturbing you. Sit silently, listen to all that is happening all around, and relax. Accept, relax – then suddenly you will feel immense energy arising in you. That energy will be felt first as the deepening of your breath. Ordinarily your breath is very shallow, and sometimes if you try to have deep breaths, you start doing *pranayam*, you start forcing something, you make an effort. That effort is not needed. Simply accept life, relax, and suddenly you will see that your breath is going deeper than ever. Relax more and the breath goes deeper in you. It becomes slow, rhythmic, and you can almost enjoy it; it gives a certain delight. And then you will become aware that breath is the bridge between you and the whole. Just watch. Don't do anything.

But the more you watch ... And when I say watch, don't *try* to watch; otherwise you will become tense again and you will start concentrating on the breath. Simply relax, remain relaxed, loose. And look – because what else can you do? You are there, nothing to be done, everything accepted, nothing to be denied, rejected, no struggle, no fight, no conflict, breathing going deep – what can you do? You simply watch. Remember, simply watch; don't make an effort to watch. This is what Buddha has called *vipassana*, the watching of the breath, awareness of the breath, or *satipatthana*, remembering, being alert of the life energy that moves in breath. Don't try to take deep breaths, don't try to inhale or exhale – don't do anything. Simply relax and let the breathing be natural – going on its own, coming on its own – and many things will become available to you.

The first thing will be that breathing can be taken in two ways, because it is a bridge: one part of it is joined with you, another part is joined with existence. So it can be understood in two ways. You can take it as a voluntary thing. If you want to inhale deeply you can inhale deeply, if you want to exhale deeply you can exhale deeply. You can do something about it, one part is joined with you. But if you don't do anything then too it continues: no need for you to do anything and it continues; it is also involuntary. The other part is joined with existence itself.

You can think of it as *you* are taking it in, you are breathing it, or you can think in just the opposite way: that it is breathing you. And the other way has to be understood because that will lead you into deep relaxation. It is not that you are breathing, but existence is breathing you. It is a change of gestalt and it happens on its own. If you go on relaxing, accepting everything, relaxing into yourself, suddenly, by and by, you become aware that you are not taking these breaths, they are coming and going on their own, and so gracefully, with such dignity, with such rhythm, with such harmonious rhythm. Who is doing it? – existence is breathing you. It comes into you, goes out of you. Each moment it rejuvenates you, each moment it makes you alive again and again and again. Suddenly you see breathing as a happening.

And this is how meditation should grow. And you can do this anywhere, in the marketplace too, because that noise is also divine. And if you listen silently, even in the marketplace you will see a certain harmony in the noise. It is no longer a distraction. You can see many things in it if you are silent; tremendous waves of energy moving all around. Once you accept, wherever you go you will feel godliness. The word is not important, but you will feel something tremendously great, you will feel something holy, something luminous, something mysterious. A miracle is constantly happening all around you but you go on missing it.

Once meditation settles in you and you fall into rhythm with existence, compassion is a consequence. Suddenly you feel you are in love with the whole and the other is no longer the other. In the other also, you live. And the tree is no longer just "that tree there"; somehow it is related with you. Everything becomes interrelated. You touch a blade of grass and you have touched all the stars, because everything is related, it cannot be otherwise. Existence is organic. It is one, it is a unity.

Because we are not aware, we don't see what we go on doing to ourselves. Touch one thing and something which you have never thought was related to it starts happening.

Just the other night I was reading something about smell. The sensation, the capacity of smell, has almost disappeared from humanity. Animals are very sharp: a horse can smell for miles, a dog can smell more than a man. Just by the smell the dog knows that his master is coming, and after years the dog will again recognize the smell that is his master's smell.

Man has completely forgotten. What has happened to smell? What calamity has happened to smell? Why? There seems to be no reason why smell has been so suppressed. No culture anywhere has consciously suppressed it, but it has become suppressed. It has become suppressed because of sex. Now the whole of humanity lives with sex deeply suppressed, and smell is connected with sex. Before making love a dog will smell the partner because unless he smells a harmony deep down between the two bodies, he will not make love. Once the smell is fitting then he knows that now the bodies are in tune and they can fit and can become a song; even for a moment a unity is possible.

Because sex has been suppressed all over the world, smell has become suppressed. The very word has become a little condemnatory. If I say to you, "Do you hear ... ?" or if I say to you, "Do you see ... ?" you don't feel offended. But if I say, "Do you smell ... ?" One should not feel offended, it is the same language. Smell is a capacity; just like seeing and hearing, smelling is a capacity. When I ask, "Do you smell ... ?" we feel offended because we have completely forgotten that it is a capacity.

There is a famous anecdote about an English thinker, Dr. Johnson. He was sitting in a stagecoach and a lady entered. She said to Dr. Johnson, "Sir, you smell!"

But he was a man of language, letters, a grammarian. He said, "No, madam. You smell. I stink!"

Smelling is a capacity. "You smell. I stink." Linguistically he is right. That's how it should be if you follow grammar. But the very word has become very condemnatory. What has happened to smell? Once you suppress sex, smell is suppressed.

You can read in the scriptures that people say, "I saw God." Nobody says, "I smelled God." What is wrong in it? If the eyes are right then why is the nose wrong? In the Old Testament it is said that your face is beautiful and your taste is beautiful, but not your smell. Smell is not talked about. We talk about God's beatific vision; we never talk about his beatific smell.

One sense is completely crippled, but if you cripple one sense then one part of the mind is crippled. If you have five senses then your mind has five parts. One fifth of the mind is crippled and one never knows – that means one fifth of life is crippled! The implications are tremendous.

If you touch a small thing somewhere, it reverberates all over. Accept everything. I was talking to you a few minutes ago about repressing sex: because of repressing sex, smell has been repressed, and because of repressing sex your breathing has become shallow – because if you breathe deeply your breathing massages the sex center inside. People come to me and say, "If we really breathe, we feel more sexual." If you make love to a woman your breathing will become very deep. If you keep your breathing shallow you will not be able to achieve orgasm. The breathing hits hard, deep down in the sex center; from the within it massages the sex center.

Because sex has been repressed, breathing is repressed, and because breathing is repressed people have become incapable of meditation. Now look at the whole thing: what nonsense we have done! Repressing sex, we have repressed breathing – and breathing is the only bridge between you and the whole.

Gurdjieff is right when he says that almost all religions have behaved in such a way that they seem to be against God. They talk about God but they seem to be basically against him. The way they have behaved is against him. Now that breathing is repressed, the bridge is broken. You can only breathe shallowly, you never go deep. And if you cannot go deep in yourself you cannot go deep in existence.

Buddha makes breathing his very foundation. A deep, relaxed breathing, an awareness of it, gives you such tremendous silence, relaxation, that by and by you simply merge, melt, disappear. You are no longer a separate island, you start vibrating with the whole. Then you are not a separate note but part of this whole symphony. Then compassion arises.

Compassion arises only when you can see that everybody is related to you. Compassion arises only when you can see that you are a member of everybody and everybody is a member of you. Nobody is separate. When the illusion of separation drops, compassion arises. Compassion is not a discipline.

In the human experience, the relationship between a mother and her child is the closest to compassion. People call it love but it should not be called love. It is more like compassion than love because it has no passion in it. A mother's love for the child is closest to compassion. Why? – because the mother has known the child in herself, he was a member of her being. She has known the child as part of herself and even if the child is born and is growing the mother goes on feeling a subtle rhythm with the child. If the child feels ill a thousand miles away, the mother will immediately feel it. She may not be aware of what has happened but she will become depressed. She may not be aware that her child is suffering but she will start suffering. She will find some rationalization about why she is suffering: her stomach is not okay, she has a headache, or something or other. But now in-depth psychology says that the mother and the child always remain joined together with subtle energy waves because they go on vibrating on the same wavelength. The telepathy is easier between a mother and the child than between anybody else – or between twins. Between twins telepathy is very easy.

Many experiments on telepathy have been done in Russia – of course, not for religion. They are trying to find out if telepathy can be used as a war technique. They will use it because they are finding clues: twins are very telepathic. If one twin has a cold, a thousand miles away the other starts having a cold. They vibrate on the same wavelength. They are affected by the same things within seconds because they have both lived in the same womb as part of each other; they have existed in the mother's womb together.

A mother's feeling for the child is more of compassion because she feels he is her own.

I was reading an anecdote:

During the preliminary inspection of a Boy Scout camp, the director found a large umbrella hidden in the bedroll of a tiny scout, obviously not one of the items of equipment listed. The director asked the lad to explain.

The tenderfoot did so neatly by asking, "Sir, did you ever have a mother?"

Mother means compassion, *mother* means feeling for the other as one feels for oneself. When a person moves deeply in meditation and attains to *samadhi*, he becomes a mother. Buddha is more like a mother than like a father. The Christian association with the word *father* is not very meaningful or beautiful. To call God *father* looks a little male-orientated. If there is any God he can only be a mother, not a father.

Father is so institutional. A father is an institution. In nature the father doesn't exist. If you ask a linguist he will say that the word *uncle* is older than the word *father*. Uncles came first into existence because nobody knew who his *father* was. Once private property was fixed, once marriage became a private ownership, the institution of fatherhood entered into human life. It is very fragile, it can disappear any day. If society changes, the institution can disappear, as many other institutions have disappeared. But the mother is going to remain – the mother is natural.

In the East many people, many traditions, have called God "the mother." Their approach seems to be more relevant. Watch Buddha: his face seems more like a woman than like a man, in fact, because of that we have not depicted him as having a beard or mustache. No, Mahavira, Buddha, Krishna, Ram – you never see any mustache or beard on their faces. Not that they were lacking in some hormones; they must have had beards, but we have not depicted them because that would give their faces a more male-like appearance. And in the East we don't bother much about facts, but we bother much about relevance, significance. Of course the statues of Buddha that you have seen are all false, but in the East we don't worry about that. The significance is that Buddha has become more womanly, more feminine. That is what I was telling you about the first day: the shift from the left hemisphere of the brain to the right hemisphere of the brain, from the male to the female; the shift from the aggressive to the passive, the shift from the positive to the negative, the shift from effort to effortlessness.

A buddha is more feminine, more motherly. If you really become a meditator, by and by, you will see many changes in your being and you will feel more like a woman than like a man – more graceful, more receptive, nonviolent, loving. And a compassion will arise continuously from your being; it will be just a natural fragrance.

Ordinarily whatsoever you call compassion goes on hiding your passion in it. Even if you sometimes feel sympathetic towards people, watch, dissect, go deeper into your feeling and somewhere you will find some motivation. In acts which look very compassionate, deep down you will always find some motivation.

Once it happened that a man called Louie came back home. He was very shocked to find his wife in the arms of another man. He rushed out of the room crying, "I am getting my shotgun."

His wife dashed after him despite her unclothed state, seized him and shouted, "You fool, what are you getting excited about? It was my lover who paid for the new furniture we recently got, my new clothes, the extra money you thought I earned sewing, all the little luxuries we have been able to buy – they all came from him!"

But Louie wrenched himself away and continued upstairs.

"No shotgun, Louie!" yelled his wife.

"What shotgun?" called back Louie. "I am getting a blanket. That poor fellow will catch cold, lying there like that."

Even if you feel – or you think you feel or you pretend that you feel – compassion, just go deeply and analyze it and you will always find some other motivation in it. It cannot be pure compassion, and if it is not pure, it is not compassion because purity is a basic ingredient in compassion. Otherwise it is something else; it is more or less a formality. We have learned how to be formal: how to behave with your wife, how to behave with your husband, how to behave with your children, with friends, with your family. We have learned everything. Compassion is not something which can be learned. When you have unlearned all formalities, all etiquette and manners, it arises in you. It is very wild. It doesn't taste of etiquette, of formality – they are all dead things compared to it. It is very alive, it is a flame of love.

At the twelfth hole of a hotly-contested match, the grounds overlooked the highway and as Smith and Jones approached the green, they saw a funeral procession making its way along the road.

At this, Smith stopped, took off his hat, placed it over his heart and bent his head till the procession disappeared around the bend.

Jones was astonished, and after Smith had replaced his hat and returned to his game, he said, "That was delicate and respectful of you, Smith."

"Ah, well," said Smith, "I could not do less. I had been married to the woman for twenty years, after all."

Life has become plastic, artificial, formal, because you have to do certain things that you do. Reluctantly of course you follow duties. But if you miss much of life it is natural, because life is possible only if you are alive, intensely alive. If your own flame has become covered by formalities, duties, rules, which you have to fulfill reluctantly, you can only drag. You may drag comfortably, your life may be a life of convenience, but it cannot be really alive.

A really alive life is, in a way, chaotic. In a way, I say, because that chaos has its own discipline. It has no rules because it need not have any rules. It has the most basic rule in-built in it: it need not have any external rules.

Now the Zen story:

One winter day, a masterless samurai came to Eisai's temple and made an appeal: I'm poor and sick," he said, "and my family is dying of hunger. Please help us, master."
Dependent as he was on widows' mites, Eisai's life was very austere, and he had nothing to give. He was about to send the samurai off when he remembered the image of Yakushi-Buddha in the hall. Going up to it he tore off its halo and gave it to the samurai. "Sell this," said Eisai, "it should tide you over."
The bewildered but desperate samurai took the halo and left.
"Master!" cried one of Eisai's disciples, "that's sacrilege! How could you do such a thing?"
"Sacrilege? Bah! I have merely put the Buddha's mind, which is full of love and mercy, to use, so to speak. Indeed, if he himself had heard that poor samurai, he would have cut off a limb for him."

A very simple story, but very significant.

First, even when you have nothing to give, look again: you will always find something to give. Even when you have nothing to give you can always find something to give. It is a question of attitude: if you cannot give anything at least you can smile, if you cannot give anything at least you can sit with the person and hold his hand. It is not a question of giving something, it is a question of giving.

This Eisai was a poor monk, as Buddhist monks are. His life was very austere and he had nothing to give. Ordinarily, it is an absolute sacrilege to take the halo off Buddha's statue and give it away. No so-called religious person could think of it, unless it is somebody who is really religious. That's why I say compassion knows no rules, compassion is beyond rules. It is wild, it follows no formalities.

Then suddenly the master remembered the image of Buddha in the hall. In Japan, in China, they put a gold halo around the head of the Buddha, just to show the aura around his head. Suddenly the master remembered it – every day he must have worshipped the same statue.

> Going up to it he tore off its halo and gave it to the samurai. "Sell this," said Eisai, "it should tide you over."
> The bewildered but desperate samurai took the halo and left.

Even the samurai was bewildered. He had not expected this. Even he must have thought that this was sacrilege: "What type of man is this? He is a follower of Buddha and he has destroyed the statue. Even to touch the statue is sacrilege and he has taken away the halo."

This is the difference between a real religious person and a so-called religious person. The so-called religious person always looks to the rule, he always thinks of what is proper and what is not proper. But a really religious person lives it; there is nothing proper and improper for him. Compassion is so infinitely proper that whatsoever you do through compassion automatically becomes proper.

> "Master!" cried one of Eisai's disciples, "that's sacrilege! How could you do such a thing?"

Even a disciple understands that this is not right. Something improper has been done.

> "Sacrilege? Bah! I have merely put the Buddha's mind, which is full of love and mercy, to good use, so to speak. Indeed, if he himself had heard that poor samurai, he would have cut off a limb for him."

To understand is something other than just to follow. When you follow you become almost blind. Then there are rules which have to be kept. But if you understand then too you follow, but you are no longer blind. And each moment decides; each moment your consciousness responds and whatsoever you do is right.

One of the most beautiful stories in Zen is about a Zen master who asked, one winter night, to be allowed to stay in a temple. He was shivering because the night was cold and snow was falling outside. Of course, the temple priest sympathized and told him, "You can stay, but only for the night, because this temple is not a *sarai*. In the morning you will have to go."

In the middle of the night the priest suddenly heard a noise. He came running and could not believe his eyes. The monk was sitting around a fire which he had made inside the temple — and one Buddha statue was missing.

In Japan they make wooden Buddha statues.

The priest asked, "Where is the statue?"

The master showed him the fire and he said, "I was shivering and it is very cold."

The priest said, "You seem to be mad! Don't you see what you have done? It was a Buddha statue. You have burned Buddha!"

The master looked in the fire, which was disappearing, and poked the fire with a stick.

The priest asked, "What are you doing?"

He said, "I am trying to find the bones of the Buddha."

The priest said, "You are certainly mad. It is a wooden Buddha, there are no bones in it."

Then the monk said, "The night is still long and it is getting even colder. Why not bring these two other Buddhas too?"

Of course, he had to be thrown out of the temple immediately — this man was dangerous!

When he was being thrown out he said, "What are you doing? — throwing a live buddha out for a wooden Buddha? The alive buddha was suffering so much, I had to show compassion. And if Buddha were alive he would have done the same. He would himself have given all those three statues to me. I know it. I know it from my very heart that he would have done the same!"

But who was there to listen to him? He was thrown out into the snow and the doors were closed.

In the morning, when the priest went out, he saw the master sitting near a milestone with a few flowers on top of it, worshipping it. The priest came again and said, "What are you doing now? Worshipping a milestone?"

The master said, "Whenever the time to pray comes, I create my Buddhas anywhere, because they are always all around. This milestone is as good as your wooden Buddhas inside the temple!"

It is a question of attitude. When you look with worshipful eyes, then anything becomes divine.

And remember, the story about Eisai is easy to understand because the compassion is shown towards somebody else. The other story is even more complex and difficult to understand because the compassion is shown towards oneself. A real man of understanding is neither hard towards others nor hard towards himself, because it is one and the same energy. A real man of understanding is not a masochist. He is not a sadist, he is not a masochist. A real man of understanding simply understands that there is no separation: all, including himself, is divine – and he lives out this understanding.

To live out of understanding is compassion. Never try to practice it, simply relax deep into meditation. Be in a state of let-go in meditation and suddenly you will be able to smell the fragrance that is coming from your own innermost depth. Then the flower blossoms and compassion spreads. Meditation is the flower and compassion is its fragrance.

Enough for today.

Chapter 4

Be a Light unto Yourself

❓ Is Zen the path of surrender? Then how come the basic teaching of Buddha is, "Be a light unto yourself"?

The essential surrender happens within you. It has nothing to do with anybody outside you. The basic surrender is a relaxation, a trust — so don't be misguided by the word. Linguistically, *surrender* means to surrender to somebody, but religiously, surrender simply means trust, relaxing. It is an attitude rather than an act: you live through trust.

Let me explain. You swim in water, you go to the river and swim. What do you do? — you trust water. A good swimmer trusts so much that he almost becomes one with the river. He is not fighting, he does not grab the water, he is not stiff and tense. If you are stiff and tense you will be drowned, if you are relaxed the river takes care.

That's why whenever somebody dies, the dead body floats on the water. This is a miracle. Amazing! Alive, the person died and was drowned by the river, but dead, the person simply floats on the surface. What has happened? The dead person knows some secret about the river which the alive person did not know. The alive person was fighting. The river was the enemy. He was afraid, he could not trust. But the dead person, not being there, how could he fight? The dead person is totally relaxed, with no tension: suddenly the body surfaces, the river takes care. No river can drown a dead person.

Trust means you are not fighting. Surrender means you don't think of life as the enemy but as the friend. Once you trust the river, suddenly you start enjoying. Tremendous delight arises: splashing, swimming, or just floating or diving deep. But you are not separate from the river, you merge, you become one.

Surrender means to live the same way in life as a good swimmer swims in the river. Life is a river: either you can fight or you can float, either you can push the river and try to go against the current or you can float with the river and go wherever the river leads you.

Surrender is not towards somebody, it is simply a way of life. A God is not needed to surrender to. There are religions which believe in God, there are religions which don't believe in any God — but all religions believe in surrender, so surrender is the real God.

Even the concept of God can be discarded. Buddhism does not believe in any God, Jainism does not believe in any God, but they are religions. Christianity believes in God, Islam believes in God, Sikhism believes in God; they are also religions. The Christian teaches surrender to God: God is just an excuse to surrender. It is a help because it will be difficult for you to surrender without any object. The object is just an excuse so that in the name of God you can surrender. Buddhism says simply, "Surrender: there is no God. Relax. It is not a question of some object, it is a question of your own subjectivity. Relax, don't fight, accept."

The belief in God is not needed. In fact, the word *belief* is ugly; it does not show trust, it does not show faith. Belief is almost the very opposite of faith. The word *belief* comes from a root *lief*. *Lief* means to desire, to wish. Now let me explain it to you. You say, "I believe in God, the compassionate" – what exactly are you saying? You are saying, "I wish there was a God who is compassionate." Whenever you say, "I believe," you say, "I intensely desire" but you don't know.

If you know there is no question of belief. Do you believe in the trees here? Do you believe in the sun which rises every morning? Do you believe in the stars? There is no question of belief. You know that the sun is there, that the trees are there. Nobody believes in the sun; if he did you would say he is mad. If somebody came and said, "I believe in the sun," and tried to convert you, you would say, "You have gone mad!"

I have heard an anecdote:

A certain lady, Lady Lewis, was appointed ambassador to Italy by the United States of America. She was a recently converted Catholic, and of course, when people become converted they are very enthusiastic. And she was boring everybody. Whosoever she came into contact with, she would try to make him a Catholic.

The story goes that when she went to Italy as the ambassador, she went to see the pope. A long discussion followed, it went on and on. A press reporter slipped closer and closer just to hear what was going on. The pope had never given so much time to anybody, and the discussion seemed to be very heated and hot. Something was going on. When the pope talks so long to the ambassador of the richest and the strongest nation in the world, there is going to be some news.

Just to overhear he came closer and closer. He could hear only one sentence. The pope was saying in a faltering English, "Lady, you don't understand me. I am already a Catholic!"

She was trying to convert the pope!

If somebody comes and says to you, "Believe in the sun," you will say, "I am already a Catholic. I already believe. Don't be worried about it" – because you know.

Somebody asked Sri Aurobindo, "Do you believe in God?"

He said, "No."

Of course the questioner was very shocked. He had come from far away, from Germany, and he was a great seeker of God and he was hoping for much, and this man simply says a flat no. He said, "But I was thinking that you have known him."

Aurobindo said, "Yes, I have known him, but I don't believe in him."

Once you know, what is the point of belief? Belief is in ignorance. If you know, you know. And it is good if you don't know, to know that you don't know. The belief can deceive you. The belief can create an atmosphere in your mind where without knowing you start thinking that you know. Belief is not trust, and the more strongly you say that you believe totally the more you are afraid of the doubt within you.

Trust knows no doubt. Belief is just repressing doubt; it is a desire. When you say, "I believe in God," you are saying, "I cannot live without God. It will be too difficult to exist in this darkness, surrounded by death, without a concept of God." That concept helps. One doesn't feel alone, one doesn't feel unprotected, insecure – hence belief.

Martin Luther has written, "My God is a great fortress." These words cannot come from a man who trusts. "My God is a great fortress"? Martin Luther seems to be on the defensive. Even God is just a fortress to protect you, to make you feel secure? – then it is out of fear. The thinking: "God is my greatest fortress" is born out of fear, not out of love. It is not of trust. Deep down there is doubt and fear.

Trust is simple. It is just like a child trusting in his mother. It is not that he believes, belief has not yet entered. You were a small child once. Did you believe in your mother or did you trust her? The doubt has not arisen, so what is the question of belief? Belief comes only when the doubt has entered; doubt comes first. Later on, to suppress the doubt, you catch hold of a belief. Trust is when doubt disappears, trust is when doubt is not there.

For instance, you breathe. You take a breath in, then you exhale, you breathe out. Are you afraid of breathing out because who knows, it may come back, it may not come back? You trust. You trust that it will come. Of course there is no reason to trust. What is the reason? Why should it come back? You can, at the most, say that in the past it has been happening so, but that is not a guarantee. It may not happen in the future. If you become afraid of breathing out because it may not come back, then you will hold your breath in. That's what belief is: clinging, holding. But if you hold your breath in, your face will go purple and you will feel suffocated. And if you go on doing that you will die.

All beliefs suffocate and all beliefs help you not to be really alive. They deaden your being.

You exhale, you trust in life. The Buddhist word *nirvana* simply means exhaling, breathing out, trusting. Trust is a very, very innocent phenomenon. Belief is of the head, trust is of the heart. One simply trusts life because you are out of life, you live in life and you will go back again to the source. There is no fear. You are born, you live, you will die; there is no fear. You will be born again, you will live again, you will die; it is a wheel. The same life that has given you life can always give you more life, so why be afraid?

Why cling to beliefs? Beliefs are manmade, trust is God-made. Beliefs are philosophical, trust has nothing to do with philosophy. Trust simply shows that you know what love is. It is not a concept of God who is sitting somewhere in heaven and manipulating and managing. Trust needs no God: this infinite life, this totality, is more than enough. Once you trust you relax. That relaxation is surrender.

Now, "Is Zen the path of surrender?" Yes. Religion, as such, is surrendering, relaxing. Don't cling to anything. Clinging shows that you don't trust life.

Every evening, Mohammed used to distribute whatsoever he had collected in the day. All! Not even a single *pai* would he save for the next day, because he said, "The same source that has given today will give me tomorrow. If it has happened today, why be untrusting about tomorrow? Why save?"

But when he was dying and he was very ill, his wife became worried. Even at midnight a physician might be needed, so that evening she saved five *rupees*, five *dinars*. She was afraid. "Nobody knows. He may become too ill in the night and some medicine may be needed. And where will I go in the middle of the night? Or a doctor may be needed and the fee will have to be given." Not saying anything to Mohammed, she saved five dinars.

Nearabout midnight, Mohammed opened his eyes and he said, "I feel a certain distrust around me. It seems something has been saved."

The wife became very much afraid and she said, "Excuse me, but thinking that something may be needed in the night, I have saved just five dinars."

Mohammed said, "Go out and give it to somebody."

She said, "Who is going to be there in the middle of the night?"

Mohammed said, "Just listen and let me die peacefully, otherwise I will feel guilty, guilty against my God. And if he asks me, I will feel ashamed that at the last moment I died in deep distrust. Go out!"

The wife went out, unbelieving of course, but a beggar was standing there.

When she came back Mohammed said, "Look, he manages well, and if we need something then a donor will be standing outside the door. Don't be worried."

Then he pulled up his blanket and died immediately. He relaxed totally.

Clinging to anything, anything whatsoever, shows distrust. If you love a woman or a man and you cling, that simply shows that you don't trust. If you love a woman and you say, "Will you also love me tomorrow or not?" you don't trust. If you go to the court to get married you don't trust. Then you trust more in the court, in the police, in the law, than in love. You are preparing for tomorrow. If this woman or this man tries to deceive you tomorrow or leaves you in the ditch, you can get support from the court and the police, and the law will be with you and the whole society will support you. You are making arrangements, afraid.

But if you really love, love is enough, more than enough. Who bothers about tomorrow? But deep down there is doubt. Even while you think you are in love, doubt continues.

It is reported that when Jesus was resurrected after his crucifixion, the first person to see him back alive was Mary Magdalene. She had loved him tremendously. She ran towards him. In the New Testament it is said that Jesus said, "Don't touch me."

I became a little suspicious because Jesus saying, "Don't touch me," does not look right. Something somewhere has gone wrong. Of course, it is okay if a pope says, "Don't touch me," but a Jesus saying, "Don't touch me"? Almost impossible!

So I tried to find the original. In the original there is a word, a Greek word, that can mean both touch or cling. Then I found the key. Jesus says, "Don't cling to me," not "Don't touch me," but the translators have interpreted it as, "Don't touch me." The interpreter has entered his own mind in it. Jesus must have said, "Don't cling to me," because if there is trust there is no clinging. If there is love there is no clinging. You simply share without any clinging, you share in deep relaxation.

Surrendering means surrendering to life, surrendering to the source from where you come and to where one day you will go back again. You are just like a wave in the ocean: you come out of the ocean, you go back to the ocean. Surrendering means trusting in the ocean. And of course, what can a wave do except that? The wave has to trust the ocean – and whether you trust or not you remain part of the ocean. Non-trusting, you will create anxiety, that's all. Nothing will change, only you will become anxious, tense, desperate. If you trust, you flower, you bloom, you celebrate, knowing well that deep down is your mother, the ocean. When tired you will go back and rest in her being again. When rested you will come back again to have a taste of the sky and the sunlight and the stars. Surrendering is trusting and it has nothing to do with any concept of God, any ideology of God. It is an attitude.

Then you can understand the meaning of Buddha's last utterance: "Be a light unto yourself." When he says be a light unto yourself he means: If you have surrendered to life you have become a light unto yourself. Then life leads you. Then you always live in enlightenment. When he says "Be a light unto yourself" he is saying don't follow anybody, don't cling to anybody. Learn from everybody but don't cling to anybody. Be open, vulnerable, but remain on your own, because finally the religious experience cannot be a borrowed experience. It has to be existential, it has to be your own. Only then is it authentic.

If I say something and you believe in it, it is not going to help. If I say something and you search and you surrender and you trust, then you also experience the same – then it has become a light unto yourself. Otherwise my words will remain words; at the most they can become beliefs. Unless you experience the truth of them they cannot become trust, they cannot become your own truth. My truth cannot be yours, otherwise it would have been very cheap. If my truth could be yours then there would be no problem.

That is the difference between a scientific truth and a religious truth. A scientific truth can be borrowed. A scientific truth, once known, becomes everybody else's property. Albert Einstein discovered the theory of relativity. Now there is no need for everybody to discover it again and again and again. That would be foolish. Once discovered, it has become public. Now it is everybody's theory. Once discovered, once proved, now even a schoolchild can learn it. Now no genius is needed: you need not be an Albert Einstein, just a mediocre mind will do, just an ordinary mind will do. You can understand it and it is yours. Of course, Einstein had to work for years, then he was able to discover it. You need not work. If you are ready to understand and put your mind to it, in just a few hours you will understand.

But the same is not true about religious truth. Buddha discovered, Christ discovered, Nanak and Kabir discovered, but their discovery cannot become *your* discovery. You will have to rediscover it again. You will have to move again from *ABC*, you cannot just believe in them. That won't help. But that is what humanity has been doing: mistaking religious truth for scientific truth. It is not scientific truth, it can never become public property. Each individual has to come to it alone, each individual has to come to it again and again. It can never become available in the market. You will have to pass through the hardship; you will have to seek and search, you will have to follow the same path. A shortcut cannot even be made. You will have to pass through the same austerities as Buddha, the same difficulties as the Buddha, and you will have to suffer the same calamities on the path as the Buddha and you will have to be in the same hazards as the Buddha. And one day, when the clouds disappear, you will dance and be as ecstatic as the Buddha.

Of course, when an Archimedes discovers, he runs naked in the streets: "Eureka! I have found it!" You can understand Archimedes within minutes, within seconds, but you will not be ecstatic; otherwise every schoolchild would run naked in the streets, crying, "Eureka!" Nobody has done that since Archimedes did it; it happened only once. For Archimedes it was a discovery, since then it has become public property.

But it is good that the religious truth cannot be transferred to you, otherwise you would never achieve the same ecstasy as Buddha or Jesus or Krishna, never, because you would learn it in a school textbook. Any fool could transfer it to you. Then the whole orgasmic experience will be lost.

It is good that religious experience has to be experienced individually. Nobody can lead you there. People can indicate the way and those indications are very subtle. Don't take them literally. Buddha said, "Be a light unto yourself." He is saying, "Remember, my truth cannot be your truth, my light cannot be your light. Imbibe the spirit from me, become more thirsty from me. Let your search be intense and be totally devoted to it. Learn the devotion of a truth-seeker from me but the truth, the light, will burn within *you*. You will have to kindle it within you."

You cannot borrow truth. It cannot be transferred, it is not a property. It is such a subtle experience that it cannot even be expressed. It is inexpressible. One, at the most, tries to give a few hints.

❓ Please explain the nature of the experiences we call "boredom" and "restlessness."

Boredom and restlessness are deeply related. Whenever you feel boredom, then you feel restlessness. Restlessness is a byproduct of boredom.

Try to understand the mechanism. Whenever you feel bored you want to move away from that situation. If somebody is saying something and you are getting bored, you start becoming fidgety. This is a subtle indication that you want to move from this place, from this man, from this nonsense talk. Your body starts moving. Of course, because of politeness you suppress it, but the body is already on the move — because the body is more authentic than the mind, the body is more honest and sincere than the mind. The mind is trying to be polite, smiling. You say, "How beautiful," but inside you are saying, "How horrible! I have listened to this story so many times and he is telling it again!"

I have heard about Albert Einstein's wife, Frau Einstein. A friend of Albert Einstein used to come many times and Einstein would tell some anecdotes, some jokes, and they would laugh. The friend became curious about one thing: whenever he came, and whenever Einstein would start telling jokes …

Einstein was a Jew, and Jews have the best jokes in the world. Because they have suffered so long they have lived by jokes. Their life has been so miserable that they had to tickle themselves; hence they have the most beautiful jokes. No other country, no other race, can compete with them. In India we don't have good jokes at all because the country has lived very peacefully – no need to tickle. Humor is needed when one is in constant danger: one needs to laugh at anything, any excuse will do to laugh.

Einstein would tell some joke, some anecdote, some story, and they both would laugh. But the friend became curious because whenever Einstein would start saying something, the wife would immediately start knitting or doing something.

So he asked, "The moment Einstein starts telling some joke, why do you start knitting?"

The wife said, "If I don't do anything, it will be tremendously difficult for me to tolerate because I have heard that joke a thousand and one times. You come sometimes, I am always here. Whenever anybody comes he tells the same joke. If I didn't do something with my hands I would become so fidgety that it would be almost impolite. So I have to do something so that I can move my restlessness into work and I can hide behind the work."

Whenever you feel bored you will feel restless. Restlessness is an indication of the body. The body is saying, "Move away from here. Go anywhere, but don't be here." But the mind goes on smiling and the eyes go on sparkling, and you go on saying that you are listening and you have never heard such a beautiful thing. The mind is civilized, the body is still wild. The mind is human, the body is still animal. The mind is false, the body is true. The mind knows the rules and regulations – how to behave and how to behave rightly – so even if you meet a bore you say, "I am so happy, so glad to see you!" And deep down, if you were allowed you would kill this man. He tempts you to murder. Then you become fidgety, then you feel restlessness.

If you listen to the body and run away, the restlessness will disappear. Try it. Try it! If somebody is boring simply start jumping and running around. See: restlessness will disappear because restlessness simply shows that the energy does not want to be here. The energy is already on the move, the energy has already left this place. Now you follow energy.

So the real thing is to understand boredom, not restlessness. Boredom is a very, very significant phenomenon. Only man feels bored, no other animal. You cannot make a buffalo bored – impossible! Only man gets bored because only man is conscious. Consciousness is the cause. The more sensitive you are, the more alert you are, the more conscious you are, the more you will feel bored. You will feel bored in more situations. A mediocre mind does not feel so bored. He goes on, he accepts: whatsoever is, is okay; he is not so alert. The more alert you become, the more fresh, the more you will feel it if some situation is just a repetition, if some situation is just getting hard on you, if some situation is just stale. The more sensitive you are the more bored you will become.

Boredom is an indication of sensitivity. Trees are not bored, animals are not bored, rocks are not bored, because they are not sensitive enough. This has to be one of the basic understandings about your boredom: that you are sensitive.

But buddhas are also not bored. You cannot bore a buddha. Animals are not bored and buddhas are not bored, so boredom exists as a middle phenomenon between the animal and the buddha. For boredom, a little more sensitivity is needed than is given to the animal. And if you want to get beyond it then you have to become totally sensitive – then again the boredom disappears. But in the middle the boredom is there. Either you become animal-like, then boredom disappears ...

So you will find that people who live a very animalistic life are less bored. Eating, drinking, making merry, they are not very bored – but they are not sensitive. They live at the minimum. They live only with that much consciousness as is needed for a day-to-day routine life. You will find that intellectuals, people who think too much, are more bored, because they think. And because of their thinking they can see that something is just stale repetition.

Your life is repetition. Every morning you get up almost the same way as you have been getting up all your life. You take your breakfast almost the same way. Then you go to the office – the same office, the same people, the same work. Then you come home – the same wife. If you get bored it is natural. It is very difficult for you to see any newness here. Everything seems to be old, dust covered.

I have heard an anecdote:

Mary Jane, the very good friend of a wealthy broker, opened the door cheerfully one day, and then quickly attempted to close it when she discovered the person on the threshold to be her lover's wife.

The wife leaned against the door and said, "Oh, let me in, dear. I don't intend to make a scene, just to have a small, friendly discussion."

With considerable nervousness Mary Jane let her enter, then said cautiously, "What do you want?"

"Nothing much," said the wife, looking about. "I just want the answer to one question. Tell me dear, just between us, what do you see in that dumb jerk?"

The same husband every day becomes a dumb jerk. The same wife every day – you almost forget how she looks. If you are told to close your eyes and to remember your wife's face, you will find it impossible to remember. Many other women will come into your mind, the whole neighborhood, but not your wife.

The relationship has become a continuous repetition. You make love, you hug your wife, you kiss your wife, but these are all empty gestures now. The glory and the glamour have disappeared long ago.

A marriage is almost finished by the time the honeymoon is over. Then you go on pretending, but behind those pretensions a deep boredom accumulates. Watch people walking on the street and you will see them completely bored. Everybody is bored, bored to death. Look at their faces – no aura of delight; look at their eyes – dust-covered, no glimmer of inner happiness. They move from the office to the home, from the home to the office, and by and by their whole life becomes a mechanical routine, a constant repetition. And one day they die. Almost always people die without ever having been alive.

Bertrand Russell is reported to have said, "When I remember, I cannot find more than a few moments in my life when I was really alive, aflame." Can you remember how many moments in your life you were really aflame? It rarely happens. One dreams about those moments, one imagines those moments, hopes for those moments, but they never happen. Even if they happen, sooner or later they also become repetitive. When you fall in love with a woman or a man you feel a miracle, but by and by the miracle disappears and everything settles into a routine.

Boredom is the consciousness of repetition. Because animals cannot remember the past, they cannot feel bored. They cannot remember the past so they cannot feel the repetition. The buffalo goes on eating the same grass every day with the same delight. You cannot; how can you eat the same grass with the same delight? You get fed up.

Hence people try to change. They move into a new house, they bring a new car home, they divorce the old husband, they find a new love affair, but again that thing is going to become repetitive sooner or later. Changing places, changing persons, changing partners, changing houses, is not going to do anything. And whenever a society becomes very bored, people start moving from one town to another, from one job to another, from one wife to another. But sooner or later they realize that this is all nonsense because the same thing is going to happen again and again with every woman, with every man, with every house, with every car.

What to do then? Become more conscious. It is not a question of changing situations; transform your being, become more conscious. If you become more conscious you will be able to see that each moment is new. But for that, very much energy, tremendous energy of consciousness is needed.

The wife is not the same, remember. You are in an illusion. Go back home and look again at your wife. She is not the same. Nobody can be the same, just appearances deceive. These trees are not the same as they were yesterday. How can they be? They have grown, many leaves have fallen, new leaves have come. Look at the almond tree, how many new leaves have come! Every day the old is falling and the new is coming, but you are not that conscious.

Either have no consciousness – then you cannot feel repetition – or have so much consciousness that in each repetition you can see something new. These are the two ways to get out of boredom.

Changing outside things is not going to help. It is just like arranging the furniture in your room again and again. Whatsoever you do – you can put it this way or that way – it is the same furniture. There are many housewives who continuously think about how to manage things, how to put things, where to put them, where not to put – and they go on changing. But it is the same room, it is the same furniture. How long will you deceive yourself in this way?

A brief television skit I once saw was of a caveman and a cavewoman who were kissing wildly and hysterically. They broke apart only to say, "Gee, this is great!" Then they turned to kissing again.

Finally the cavewoman pulled away to say, "Listen, do you suppose this wonderful thing we have discovered means that we are married?"

The caveman bent his small mind to the matter and finally said, "Yes, I guess we are married. Now let us kiss some more."

Whereupon the cavewoman put her hand to her head and said in sudden anguish, "Oh, I have such a headache!"

Two persons meet, strangers, everything is wonderful, beautiful, but sooner or later they become acquainted with each other. That's what marriage means. It means that now they are settling, now they would like to make it a repetition. Then the same kissing and the same hugging is no longer beautiful, it becomes almost a duty.

A man came home and found his friend kissing his wife. He took the friend into another room. The friend was trembling with fear: "Now there is going to be something! The friendship will be broken."

The husband seemed to be very angry, but he was not. He closed the door and asked the friend, "Just tell me one thing: I *have* to, but why were you kissing her?"

"I *have* to, but why were you kissing her?" By and by everything settles. Newness disappears, and you don't have that much consciousness or that quality of consciousness which can go on finding the new again and again. For a dull mind everything is old, for a totally alive mind there is nothing old under the sun – there cannot be. Everything is in flux. Every person is in flux, is river-like. Persons are not dead things – how can they be the same? Are you the same?

Between when you came this morning to listen to me and when you will go back home, a lot has happened. Some thoughts have disappeared from your mind, some other thoughts have entered your mind. You may have attained to a new insight. You cannot go the same as you had come. The river is continuously flowing; it looks the same but it is not the same. Old Heraclitus has said that you cannot step twice into the same river, because the river is never the same.

One thing is that you are also not the same, and another thing is that everything is changing. But then one has to live at the peak of consciousness. Either live like a buddha or live like a buffalo, then you will not be bored. Now the choice is yours.

I have never seen anybody the same. You come to me – how many times you have come to me – but I never see the old. I'm always surprised by the newness that you bring every day. You may not be aware of it.

Remain capable of being surprised.

Let me tell you one anecdote:

A man entered a bar, deep in private thoughts of his own. He turned to a woman just passing and said, "Pardon me, miss, do you happen to have the time?"

In a strident voice she responded, "How dare you make such a proposition to me!"

The man snapped to attention in surprise and was uncomfortably aware that every pair of eyes in the place had turned in their direction. He mumbled, "I just asked the time, miss."

In a voice even louder the woman shrieked. "I will call the police if you say another word!"

Grabbing his drink and embarrassed very nearly to death, the man hastened to the far end of the room and huddled at a table, holding his breath and wondering how soon he could sneak out the door.

No more than half a minute had passed when the woman joined him. In a quiet voice she said, "I'm terribly sorry, sir, to have embarrassed you, but I am a psychology student at the university and I am writing a thesis on the reaction of human beings to sudden, shocking statements."

The man stared at her for three seconds, then he leaned back and bellowed, "You will do all that for me, all night, for just two dollars?"

And it is said that the woman fell down, unconscious.

Maybe we don't allow our consciousness to rise higher because then life will be a constant surprise and you may not be able to manage it. That's why you have settled for a dull mind – there is some investment in it. You are not dull for no reason. You are dull for a certain purpose, because if you are really alive then everything will be surprising and shocking. If you remain dull then nothing surprises you, nothing is shocking. The more dull you are, the more life seems to be dull to you. If you become more aware, life will also become more alive, livelier, and there is going to be difficulty.

You always live with dead expectations. Every day you come home and you expect a certain behavior from your wife. Now look how you create your own misery: you expect a certain fixed behavior from your wife and then you expect your wife to be new. You are asking the impossible. If you really want your wife to remain continuously new to you, don't expect. Come home always ready to be surprised and shocked, then the wife will be new. But she has to fulfill certain expectations.

We never allow our total flux-like freshness to be known to the other. We go on hiding, we don't expose, because the other may not be able to understand it at all. And the wife also expects the husband to behave in a certain way, and of course, they manage the roles. We are not living life, we are living roles. The husband comes home; he forces himself into a certain role. By the time he enters the house he is no more an alive person, he is just a husband.

A husband means a certain type of expected behavior. The woman there is a wife, and the man there is a husband. Now when these two persons meet there are really four persons: the husband and wife – which are not real persons, just personas, masks, false patterns, expected behavior, duties, and all that – and the real persons hiding behind the masks. Those real persons feel bored.

But you have invested too much in your persona, in your mask. If you really want a life which has no boredom in it, drop all masks, be true. Sometimes it will be difficult, I know, but it is worth it. Be true. If you feel like loving your wife, love her; otherwise say you don't feel like it. What is happening right now is that the husband goes on making love to the wife and goes on thinking of some actress. In imagination he is not making love to this woman, in imagination he is making love to some other woman. And the same is true about the wife. Then things become boring because they are no more alive. The intensity, the sharpness, is lost.

It happened on a railway platform. Mr. Johnson had weighed himself on one of those old-fashioned penny machines that delivered a card with a fortune printed on it.

The formidable Mrs. Johnson plucked it from her husband's fingers and said, "Let me see that. Ah, it says you are firm and resolute, have a decisive personality, are a leader of men, and are attractive to women."

Then she turned over the card, studied it for a moment and said, "And they have got the weight wrong as well."

No woman can believe that her husband is attracted to other women. Now there is the whole point, the whole crux. If he is not attracted to other women, how can she expect that he will be attracted to her? If he is attracted to other women only then can he be attracted to her, because she is also a woman. The wife wants him to be attracted to her and not attracted to anybody else. The husband wants his wife to be attracted to him and not attracted to anybody else. Now this is asking something absurd. It is as if you are saying, "You are allowed to breathe only in my presence and when you go near somebody else, you are not allowed to breathe. How dare you breathe anywhere else?" Just breathe when the wife is there, just breathe when the husband is there, and don't breathe anywhere else. Of course, if you do that you will be dead and you will also not be able to breathe in front of your wife.

Love has to be a way of life. You are to be loving, only then can you love your wife and your husband. But the wife says, "No, you should not look at anybody else with a loving eye." Of course you manage, because if you don't manage it creates such nuisance. But you manage, and by and by the glimmer in your eyes disappears. If you cannot look anywhere else with love, by and by you cannot look at your own wife with love; it disappears. The same has happened to her. The same has happened to the whole of humanity. Then life is a boredom. Then everybody is waiting for death. Then there are people continuously thinking of committing suicide.

Marcel has said somewhere that the only metaphysical problem facing humanity is suicide. And it is so, because people are so bored. It is simply amazing why they don't commit suicide, how they go on living. Life doesn't seem to give anything. All meaning seems to be lost, but still people go on dragging somehow, hoping that some day some miracle will happen and everything will be put right. It never happens. You have to put it right, nobody else is going to put it right. No messiah is to come, don't wait for any messiah. You have to be a light unto yourself.

Live more authentically. Drop the masks; they are a weight on your heart. Drop all falsities. Be exposed. Of course it is going to be troublesome, but that trouble is worth it because only after that trouble will you grow and become mature. And then nothing is holding life. Each moment life reveals its newness. It is a constant miracle happening all around you; only you are hiding behind dead habits.

Become a buddha if you don't want to be bored. Live each moment as fully alert as possible, because only in full alertness will you be able to drop the mask. Otherwise you have completely forgotten what your original face is – even when you stand before the mirror in your bathroom and you are alone, when there is nobody there. Even standing before the mirror you don't see your original face in the mirror; there too you go on deceiving.

Existence is available for those who are available to existence. And then I tell you, there is no boredom. Life is infinite delight.

❓ I feel so much resistance against meditation and I don't have this desire for God that you speak about. Is this the right place for me?

If you feel much resistance against meditation it simply shows that deep down you are alert that something is going to happen which will change your total life. You are afraid of being reborn. You have invested too much in your old habits, in the old personality, in the old identity.

Meditation is nothing but trying to clean your being, trying to become fresh and young, trying to become more alive and more alert. If you are afraid of meditation it means you are afraid of life. You are afraid of awareness. And the resistance comes because you know that if you move into meditation, something is bound to happen. If you are not resisting at all it may be because you don't take meditation very seriously, you don't take meditation very sincerely. Then you can play around — what is there to be afraid of?

It is exactly because you are resisting that this is the right place for you. This is precisely the right place for you. The resistance shows that something is going to happen. One never resists without a deep cause.

You must be living a very dead life. Now you are afraid that something is becoming alive, something is changing. You resist. Resistance is an indication, resistance is a very clear indication that you have suppressed much. Now in meditation that suppression will surface, it will be released. You would also like to be released of the burden, but in that burden there are investments.

For example, you may be carrying pebbles in your hands but you think they are diamonds. And then I tell you, "Clean yourself. Drop these pebbles." Now the problem arises that they are pebbles to me and they are diamonds to you. They have become a burden and you cannot move because of them. You would like to be unburdened, so you listen to me. You would like to be unburdened, but then you are afraid that your diamonds will be lost. And they are not diamonds. Look again at your diamonds: if they were really diamonds you should be happy. If they were really diamonds you would not have come to me at all; there is no need. If you have come, it shows that you are seeking.

You may say that you are not interested in God — I am also not interested in God — but you are interested in yourself. Are you interested in yourself? Forget all about God. If you are interested in yourself, then this is precisely the place for you. If you are interested in your own wellbeing, in your own wholeness and health, if you are interested in becoming a blossomed flower, then forget all about God – because in that blossoming you will know what godliness is. When your fragrance is released then you will know what godliness is.

Godliness is your ultimate flowering, your final flowering; your destiny fulfilled is what godliness is all about.

A woman seeing Turner's pictures said once, "Making a lot of fuss over him, aren't they? I never saw anything in him myself."

And another woman said to Turner himself, "But you know, Mr. Turner, I never see sunsets like yours."

She received the mild yet devastating reply, "No. Don't you wish you could?"

When a Turner paints a sunset, of course he sees a sunset in a totally different way than you. He brings all his sensitivity, his whole being, to see it. In fact you may not have ever seen a sunset the way a painter looks at it. Turner says rightly, "Don't you wish you could?"

I am here. I know you can't see what I am talking about, but don't you wish you could? I know that many things I am saying are almost nonsense to you because to see them you will have to attain different eyes; to see them you will have to clarify your being; to see them you will have to pacify your turmoil within. I know you cannot see the green that I am seeing in the trees. Your green is bound to be very dusty because your eyes are full of dust.

It happened once that a man was staying with a friend at somebody's house. The host and the guest were standing near the window. The window was closed, and in the neighbor's house clothes were hanging out to be dried.

The host said, "These people are very dirty. Look at their clothes."

The man looked, he came closer to the window and he said, "Those clothes are not dirty. Your window glass is covered with dust."

They opened the windows and it was so: those clothes were not dirty.

Life is tremendously beautiful. It is divine. When we say life is godly we are simply saying that life is so tremendously beautiful that one feels a reverence for it, that's all. Life is so tremendously beautiful that one feels like worshipping it. That's all we mean when we say life is godly. When we say life is godly we only mean, "Don't see life as ordinary; it is extraordinary. There is tremendous potentiality, just open your eyes." I have never seen a person who is not interested in godliness – although he may not know it – because I have never seen a person who is not interested in happiness. If you are interested in happiness you are interested in godliness, if you are interested in being blissful you are interested in godliness.

Forget all about God. Just try to be blissful, and one day, when you are dancing in your inner bliss, when the inner juices are flowing, suddenly this life is no longer ordinary. Everywhere some unknown force is hiding and you will see godliness in the flowers and in the stones and in the stars. I talk to you just to plant a seed, a song, a star.

If you can become happy, you become religious. A happy person is a religious person; let that be the definition. A religious person is not one who goes to the church or the temple. If he is unhappy, he cannot be religious.

A religious person is happy. Wherever he is, he is in the temple. A happy person carries his temple around with him. I know it because I have been carrying it. I need not go to any temple. Where I am is my temple. It is a climate, it is my own inner juice overflowing. Godliness is nothing but you realized, reached, fulfilled.

Yes, I say to you, I have never seen a man who is not interested in God. There cannot be. That man is not possible. Even people who say they don't believe in God, who are atheists, are not uninterested in God. They are interested. Their denying, their saying that they don't believe may be just a trick of the mind to protect themselves, because once you allow yourself to be possessed by godliness you disappear, only godliness remains. So people who are afraid of being, of disappearing, of moving into non-being, people who are too egoistic and cannot allow their drop to drop into the ocean, say there is no ocean. That is the trick of their mind so that they can protect themselves. They are fearful people, afraid, scared of life.

If you are interested in being happy, this is the place for you. And you are already here. Nobody has brought you, nobody has forced you. You have come on your own. Some inner search that you may not be aware of has brought you here. Maybe something is in the heart and your head does not know anything about it. There are desires of which the head is completely unaware; the head is concerned only with rubbish. The heart may have brought you here. Break that resistance. And when you are here, be really here. Don't miss this opportunity.

In the New Testament the Greek word for sin is *antinomic* or *anomia*. It means to miss the point, or, as in archery, to miss the mark. The word *sin* comes from a root which means to miss the point, to miss the mark. If you are here and you miss me, that will be a sin. If you are here then why waste time? Be totally here. Drop the resistance. Or if you cannot be totally here, then go away from here – but go totally away. Then never again remember me, otherwise that will be a sin.

The word *sin* is beautiful. It has been badly corrupted by Christianity. It has nothing to do with guilt, nothing to do with something bad, evil. It has nothing to do with morality, but it has something to do with consciousness. It has nothing to do with conscience but with consciousness. If you are here, be consciously and totally here. Your unconscious heart has brought you here. Groping in the dark you have come to me, now don't miss this opportunity. Either be totally here or go away. Turn your back against me and never remember me again, because going away, if you remember me then you will not be totally there – wherever you are going. Wherever you are, be totally there. That's the only way to open the secrets and mysteries of life.

And don't be worried about whether you are interested in the concept of God or not. In fact, people who are too interested in the concept of God will not be able to know godliness.

I have come across a very beautiful book, written somewhere in the Middle Ages by a certain man known as Dionysius Exegius. His book is *Theologica Mystica*. He says in that book that the highest knowledge of God is through what he calls in Greek *agnostos*, which means unknowing. You must have heard the word *agnostic*; it comes from the same root, *agnostos*. *Agnostos* means unknowing. And this Dionysius says that God is known only by unknowing. No need to be worried about the concept; no need to accumulate knowledge, theories, doctrines about God. Forget all about the word and the theory. Simply be interested in your happiness, in your bliss, and one day you will find godliness has entered in you. It is another name for ultimate bliss.

? **I have this idea that you don't really exist. When we think that there is someone who lives in your house and who makes things happen to us, it is not really you at all. Could you tell us what this is and by the way, who is giving the discourse every morning?**

I don't know.
Enough for today.

Chapter 5

The Ultimate Secrets of Swordsmanship

*Yagyu Tajima no Kami Munenori was a teacher of swordsmanship
to the Shogun.*
*One of the personal guards of the shogun came to Tajima no Kami
one day asking to be trained in swordplay. "As I observe, you seem
to be a master of the art yourself," said the teacher. "Please tell me
to what school you belong before we enter into the relationship of
teacher and pupil."*
*The guardsman said, "I do not belong to any school, I have never
studied the art."*
*"It is no use trying to fool me," said the master. "My judging eye
never fails."*
*"I am sorry to defy, your honor," said the guard, "but I really know
nothing."*
*"If you say so then it must be true, but I am sure that you are the
master of something, so tell me about yourself."*
*"There is one thing," said the guard. "When I was a child I thought
that a samurai should never be afraid of death. So I grappled with
the problem, and now the thought of death has ceased to worry me."*
"That's it!" exclaimed the teacher.
*"The ultimate secrets of swordsmanship lie in being released from
the thought of death. You need no technical training, you are
already a master."*

The ocean is not only hidden behind the waves, it is also manifesting itself in the waves. It is there on the surface as much as it is in the depth. The depth and the surface are not two separate things; they are two polarities of the same phenomenon. The center comes to the circumference; it is as much on the circumference as it is at the center.

The divine is not only unmanifest, it is also manifest. The divine is not only the creator, it is also the creation. It is as much in this world as it is in the other world.

Just the other night a new sannyasin asked me, "Osho, can you show me the divine form?"

I told him, "All forms are divine. I have not seen a single form which is not divine. The whole existence is divine – don't divide it into profane and sacred."

All the time, what else am I doing? – showing the divine form. What else are you doing? – showing the divine form. What else is happening all over existence? The divine is spread everywhere. It is as much in the small as it is in the great; it is as much in a grass leaf as in a faraway great star.

But the mind thinks in dualities. It thinks godliness is hidden, then it tries to deny the manifest and seek the unmanifest. Now you are creating an unnecessary conflict for yourself. Godliness is here now as much as anywhere else. Godliness is as much in the seeker as in the sought. It is manifesting itself. That's why I say that the ocean is in the waves. Dig deep into the waves, dig deep into the form, and you will find the formless.

If you cannot see this it doesn't mean that godliness is not manifested, it only means that you are still blind. You have still not got the eyes that can see the obvious. Godliness is the obvious.

And this is so on every level of being: whatsoever you are, you go on broadcasting it around you. You cannot hide it. Nothing, absolutely nothing, can be hidden. There is a Zen saying: "Nothing whatsoever is hidden from of old, all is as clear as daylight." But all is not as clear as daylight for you. That doesn't mean the daylight is not there; it simply means you are standing with closed eyes. Open your eyes just a little and the darkness starts disappearing. Open your eyes and wherever you are, immediately you will be able to see as deep as existence is. Once your eyes are open, everything becomes transparent.

When you see me, you just see the surface, the waves. When you hear me, you only hear the words, not the silence hidden behind them. You see exactly that which is of no worth and you miss all that is of any worth and significance. When I see you, it is not the form, it is not the image that you see in the mirror. When I see you, I see *you*. And you are broadcasting yourself in your every gesture, in your every movement. The way you walk, the way you talk, the way you stay silent and don't talk, the way you eat, the way you sit – everything is manifesting you. Anybody who is perceptive will be able to see whether you are dark inside or whether you have kindled the flame.

It is as easy as if you pass by a house in the night, a dark night, and the house is lighted inside. Is it in any way difficult to know it is lighted? No, because from the windows and from the doors you can see the light coming out. Or if the house is in darkness and there is no light burning inside, then of course you see it, it is obvious.

The same is happening in you: whatsoever you are is being broadcasted every moment. Your neurosis is broadcasted, your enlightenment also. Your meditation is broadcasted, your madness also. You cannot hide it. All efforts to hide yourself are futile. They are stupid, ridiculous.

I was reading a book by Edmund Carpenter. He was working on a sociological project, a research project, in Borneo.

He writes: "In a small town in Borneo, professional clerks sit before open windows, reading and writing. Because people are illiterate and they cannot read and write, so for their letters, documents, or any other thing, they need the help of professional writers and readers. And I was very surprised because I noticed one who was plugging his ears with his fingers while he read aloud. I inquired and was told that this was done at the request of the listener who did not want to share his letter with the reader!"

So the reader was plugging his ears with his fingers and reading the letter loudly!

But this is what is happening in everybody's life. You go on hiding, but everything is being declared, continuously, loudly. Everything is being broad-casted; you are a continuous broadcasting station. Even while you are asleep you are broadcasting. If a buddha comes to you while you are asleep he will be able to see who you are. Even in your sleep you will be making gestures, faces, movements, uttering something. And all those things will indicate something about you, because the sleep is yours and it is bound to carry your signature.

If one becomes a little alert, one stops hiding. It is futile, it is ridiculous. Then one simply relaxes. Because of your hiding you remain tense, continuously afraid that somebody may know about you. You never expose yourself, you never live in the nude – spiritually I mean. You never live in the nude, you are always afraid. That fear cripples you and paralyzes you.

Once you understand that everything is bound to be declared – it is already being declared; the center is coming to the circumference every moment and the ocean is waving in the waves and godliness is everywhere, spread all over existence, and you are spread all over your activities – there is no point in hiding. Nothing whatsoever is hidden from of old, everything is as clear as daylight.

Then why bother? Then one relaxes. The anxiety, the tension, the anguish disappears. Suddenly you become vulnerable, no more closed. Suddenly you are open, suddenly you become inviting. And this is the point to be understood: once you are exposed to others, only then will you be exposed to yourself. If you are hiding from others, whatsoever you are hiding from others will by and by be thrown into the basement of your unconscious mind. Others may not know about it but by and by you will also forget about it.

But whenever you come within the vision of a perceptive man, everything will be revealed. That is one of the basic reasons why, in the East, the relationship of a disciple to a master is so valued: because the master is just like a ray of light, an X-ray, and the disciple exposes himself. And the more the master penetrates and knows about the disciple the more the disciple becomes aware of his own hidden treasures by and by. Trying to hide himself from others, he has become such an expert in hiding that he hides from himself also.

You don't know much about yourself. You know just a fragment about yourself, just the tip of the iceberg. Your knowledge about yourself is very limited – not only limited, it is almost irrelevant! It is so partial, it is so fragmentary, that unless you put it in the context of your whole being it carries no meaning. It is almost meaningless.

That's why you go on living without knowing yourself. And how can one live without knowing oneself? And you go on projecting things on others which have nothing to do with others; they may be just hidden forces inside you. But you don't know that they are hidden inside you, you project them onto others. Somebody looks like an egoist to you: you may be the egoist and you project. Somebody looks very angry: the anger may be inside you and the other is just like a screen – it is you projecting.

Unless you know yourself exactly, you will not be able to know what is real and what is projection. You will also not be able to know about others. Self-knowledge becomes the door of all knowledge; it is the very base. Without that foundation, all knowledge is just knowledge in appearance; deep down it is ignorance.

I have heard an anecdote:

Mistress Jones, deeply troubled, was consulting a psychiatrist.

"My husband," she said, "is convinced he is a chicken. He goes around scratching constantly, and sleeps on a large bar of wood he has fixed up as a perch."

"I see," said the psychiatrist thoughtfully. "And how long has your husband been suffering from this fixation?"

"For nearly two years now."

The psychiatrist frowned slightly and said, "But why have you waited till now to seek help?"

Mistress Jones blushed and said, "Ah well, it was so nice having a steady supply of eggs!"

Now this woman is neurotic! She thinks her husband is neurotic: whenever you think something about somebody else, watch. Don't be in a hurry, first look within. The cause may be inside you. But you don't know yourself so you go on confusing your own projections with outer realities. It is impossible to know anything real unless you have known yourself. And the only way to know oneself is to live a life of vulnerability, openness. Don't live in a closed cell. Don't hide yourself behind your mind. Come out.

Once you come out, by and by you will become aware of millions of things in you. You are not a one room apartment, you have many rooms. You are a palace, but you have become accustomed to living on the porch and you have forgotten the palace completely. Many treasures are hidden in you, and those treasures constantly go on knocking, inviting, but you are almost deaf.

This blindness, this deafness, this insensitivity, has to be broken – and nobody else can do it. If somebody else tries you will feel offended, you will feel a trespassing. It happens every day: if I try to help you, you feel you have been trespassed upon. If I try to say something true about you, you feel offended, you feel humiliated, you feel hurt, your pride is hurt. You want to listen to lies about yourself from me; you want to listen to something which helps your already fixed image. You have a very golden image about yourself which is false. It has to be shattered to pieces because once it is shattered the reality will arise. If it is not shattered, you will go on clinging to it.

You think you are religious, you think you are a great seeker. You may not be religious at all, you may be simply afraid of life. In your temples and churches cowards are hiding, afraid of life. But to accept that one is afraid of life is very humiliating, so they say they are not afraid of life, they have renounced: "Life is not worth anything. Life is only for mediocre minds." They have renounced everything for God, they are searching for God. But watch: they are trembling. They are praying on their knees, but their prayer is not of love, their prayer is not of celebration, their prayer is not a festivity. Their prayer is out of fear, and fear corrupts everything. Nobody can approach truth through fear.

You have to approach truth through fearlessness. But if you are hiding your fear behind religiousness then it will be very difficult to shatter it. You are greedy, miserly, but you go on saying that you live a very simple life. If you are hiding behind the rationalization of simplicity then it is very difficult to see that you are a miser. And a miser misses tremendously because life is for those who share, life is for those who love, life is for those who are not too clinging to things – because then they become available to persons.

To cling to a thing is to cling to something which is below you. And if you go on clinging to things which are below you, how can you soar high? It is as if you are clinging to rocks and trying to fly in the sky, or you are carrying rocks on the head and trying to climb Everest. You have to throw them away. You have to throw away those rocks, you will have to unburden yourself.

Edmund Hillary, the first man to reach to the top of Everest, says in his autobiography, "As we started reaching closer and closer, I had to leave more and more things behind. At the last moment I had to leave almost everything, because everything became such a burden."

The higher you reach, the more unburdened you need to be. So a miser cannot soar high. A miser cannot soar in love, or in prayer, or in godliness. He remains clinging to the earth; he almost remains rooted in the earth. Trees cannot fly. If you want to fly you need to be uprooted. You need to be like a white cloud with no roots anywhere, a wanderer.

But you can hide your miserable self. And you can hide your diseases behind good, beautiful terms and words. You can be very articulate and you can be very rationalizing. All these have to be broken.

And if you go on hiding, then not only do you hide your diseases, you hide your treasures also. This hiding becomes a fixation; it becomes a habit, an obsession. But I tell you, before a perceptive man, before a master who has known himself, you will be completely x-rayed. You cannot hide from somebody who has eyes. You can hide from yourself, you can hide from the world, but you cannot hide from somebody who has come to know what clarity is, what perception is. For such a man, you are absolutely on the surface.

I have heard about an American couple who were strolling along the banks of the Seine under the shadows of Notre Dame.

He was lost in silence. She said finally, "What are you thinking about, darling?"

"I was thinking, dear, that if anything happened to either of us, I would like to spend the rest of my life in Paris."

He may not be aware of what he is saying, he may have uttered this in absolute unawareness. Let me repeat it. He says, "I was thinking, dear, that if anything happened to either of us, I would like to spend the rest of my life in Paris." He wants the wife to die although he is not saying it clearly — but he has said it.

We continuously broadcast, in many ways.

Just a few days ago President Ford gave a party in honor of the Egyptian ambassador to the States. But then when he was giving the toast he forgot completely and something from the unconscious bubbled up — a slip of the tongue, we say, but it is not just a slip of the tongue. He raised the glass and said, "In honor of the great nation of Israel." To Egyptians!

Then of course he tried to mend it, to patch it, but it was too late. Deep down he wants Israel to win over the Egyptians. It bubbled up, surfaced from the unconscious.

It happened at a party. A man was leaving, but he was very diffident. He murmured to the hostess, "The meal was delicious, what there was of it."

Noting the hurt expression on his hostess' face, the guest blushed and hastened to say, "Ah, ah. And there was plenty of food, such as it was."

These are unconscious assertions; they come out of you when you are not on guard. Ordinarily you are on guard. That's why people are so tense, continuously on guard, guarding themselves. But there are moments when the tension is too much and one relaxes. One has to relax, one cannot be on guard for twenty-four hours. In those moments, things surface.

You are truer when you have drunk a little too much and things start surfacing from your unconscious. Under the influence of alcohol you are truer than you ordinarily are, because the alcohol relaxes your guard. Then you start saying things you always wanted to say, and you are not worried about anything, and you are not trying to leave any impression – you are simply being true. Drunkards are beautiful people: truer, more authentic. It is ironic that only drunkards are authentic.

The more you are clever and cunning, the more inauthentic you become. Don't hide behind screens. Come out in the sunshine. And don't be afraid that your image will be shattered. The image that you are afraid of being shattered is not worth keeping. It is better to shatter it on your own. Take a hammer and shatter it.

That's what being a sannyasin means: that you take a hammer in your hands and you shatter the old image. And you start a new life from *ABC*, from the very beginning again, as if you are born again. It is a rebirth.

Then, by and by, if you relax and you are not too worried about your image in the eyes of others, your own authentic face, original face, comes into being – the face that you had before you were born and the face that you will again have when you are dead; the original face, not the cultivated mask. With that original face you will see godliness everywhere, because with the original face you can meet with the original, with reality.

With a mask you will meet only other masks. With a mask there can never be any dialogue with reality. With a mask you remain in the relationship of "I" and "it"; reality remains behind it. When the mask is removed and you have come back home, a tremendous transformation happens. The relationship with reality is no more one of "I-it," it is of "I-thou." That "thou" is godliness.

Reality takes on a personality: you become alive here, reality becomes alive there. It has always been alive, just you were dead. It is as if you have taken chloroform: when you come back and the influence of the chloroform by and by disappears, how do you feel? It is a beautiful experience! If you have never been to the surgeon's table, go, just for the experience. For a few moments you are completely in oblivion, and then consciousness arises. Suddenly, everything becomes alive, fresh. You are coming out of the womb. Exactly the same happens when you decide to live an authentic life. Then, for the first time you understand that now you are born. Just before you were thinking and dreaming that you were alive, but you were not.

A great mathematician, Herr Gauss, was keeping vigil while his wife lay ill upstairs. And as time passed, he found himself beginning to ponder a deep problem in mathematics.

People have grooves in their mind and they move in the same grooves again and again. A mathematician has a certain track. The wife is going to die, the doctors have said that this is going to be the last night, he is keeping vigil – but the mind started moving in its old pattern, of course. He started thinking about a mathematical problem. Just see: the wife will no longer be there, it is the last night, but the mind is creating a screen of mathematics. He has completely forgotten about the wife; he has moved, he has gone far away on a journey.

As time passed he found himself beginning to ponder a deep problem in mathematics. He drew pen and paper to himself and began to draw diagrams. A servant approached and said deferentially, "Herr Gauss, your wife is dying."

And Gauss, never looking up said, "Yes, yes. But tell her to wait till I'm through."

Even the great minds are as unconscious as you are. As far as consciousness is concerned, great, small and mediocre, all sail in the same boat. Even the greatest mind lives under chloroform.

Come out of it, make yourself more alert, bring yourself together. Let one thing become a centering – a constant centering in you – and that is alertness, awareness. Do whatsoever you do, but do it consciously. And by and by consciousness accumulates and it becomes a reservoir of energy.

Now, the Zen story:

Yagyu Tajima no Kami Munenori was a teacher of swordsmanship to the shogun.

In Zen, and only in Zen, something of great importance has happened: that is, they don't make any distinction between ordinary life and religious life, rather, they have bridged them both. And they have used very ordinary skills as *upaya*, as methods for meditation. That is something of tremendous importance. Because if you don't use ordinary life as a method for meditation, your meditation is bound to become something of an escape.

In India it has happened ... And India has suffered badly. The misery that you see all around, the poverty, the horrible ugliness of it, is because India has always thought religious life to be separate from ordinary life. So people who became interested in God renounced the world. People who became interested in God closed their eyes, sat in the caves in the Himalayas, and tried to forget that the world existed. They tried to create the idea that the world is simply an illusion, illusory: a *maya*, a dream. Of course life suffered much because of it. All the greatest minds of this country became escapist and the country was left to the mediocrities. No science could evolve, no technology could evolve.

But in Japan, Zen has done something very beautiful. That's why Japan is the only country where East and West are meeting: Eastern meditation and Western reason are in a deep synthesis in Japan. Zen has created the whole situation there. In India you cannot conceive that swordsmanship can become an *upaya*, a method for meditation, but in Japan they have done it. And I see that they have brought something very new to religious consciousness.

Anything can be converted into a meditation, because the whole thing is awareness. And of course, in swordsmanship more awareness is needed than anywhere else because life will be at stake every moment. When fighting with a sword you have to be constantly alert: a single moment's unconsciousness and you will be gone. In fact, a real swordsman does not function out of his mind. He *cannot* function out of his mind because mind takes time – it thinks, calculates – and when you are fighting with a sword, where is time? There is no time. If you miss a single fragment of a second in thinking, the other will not miss the opportunity: the other's sword will penetrate into your heart or cut off your head.

So thinking is not possible, one has to function out of no-mind. One has to simply function, because the danger is so much that you cannot afford the luxury of thinking. Thinking needs an easy chair. You just relax in an easy chair and you go off on mind-trips.

But when you are fighting, and life is at stake, and the swords are shining in the sun, and at any moment some slight unawareness and the other will not lose the opportunity – you will be gone forever – there is no space for thought to appear. One has to function out of no-thought. That's what meditation is all about.

If you can function out of no-thought, if you can function out of no-mind, if you can function as a total, organic unity – not out of the head – if you can function out of your guts, it can happen to you also.

You are walking one night and suddenly a snake crosses the path. What do you do? Do you sit there and think about it? No, suddenly you jump out of the way. In fact you don't decide to jump, you don't think in a logical syllogism, "Here is a snake and wherever there is a snake there is danger, therefore, ergo, I should jump." That is not the way. You simply jump! The action is total. The action is not corrupted by thinking; it comes out of your very core of being, not out of the head. Of course when you have jumped out of the danger you can sit under a tree and think about the whole thing – that's another matter. Then you can afford the luxury.

The house catches fire: what do you do? Do you think whether to go out or not to go out, to be or not to be? Do you consult a scripture about whether it is right to do it? Do you sit silently and meditate upon it? You simply get out of the house. And you will not be worried about manners and etiquette; you will jump out of the window.

Just two nights ago a girl entered here at three o'clock in the night and started screaming in the garden. Asheesh jumped out of his bed, ran, and only then did he realize that he was naked – then he came back.

That was an act out of no-mind, without any thought. He simply jumped out of the bed, thought came later on. Thought followed, lagged behind. He was ahead of thought. Of course, it caught hold of him so he missed an opportunity. It would have become a satori, but he came back and put on his gown, missed!

Swordsmanship became one of the *upayas*, one of the basic methodologies, because the very thing is so dangerous that it doesn't allow thinking. It can lead you towards a different type of functioning, a different type of reality, a separate reality. You know of only one way to function: to think first and then to function. In swordsmanship a different type of existence becomes open to you: you function first and then you think. Thinking is no longer primary and this is the beauty. When thinking is not primary you cannot err.

You have heard the proverb "It is human to err." Yes, it is true, it is human to err because the human mind is prone to err. But when you function out of no-mind you are no longer human, you are divine, and then there is no possibility of erring – because the total never errs, only the part, only the partial goes astray. Godliness never errs, it *cannot* err, it is the whole.

When you start functioning out of nothingness, with no syllogism, with no thinking, with no conclusions ... Of course your conclusions are limited, they depend on your experience, you can err, but when you put aside all your conclusions you are putting aside all limitations also. Then you function out of your unlimited being, and it never errs.

It is said that sometimes it has happened in Japan that two Zen people who have both attained to satori through swordsmanship fight. They cannot be defeated. Nobody can be victorious because they both never err. Before the other attacks, the first has already made preparations to receive it. Before the other's sword moves to cut off his head he is already prepared to defend the attack. And the same happens with his attack. Two Zen people who have attained to satori can go on fighting for years, but it is impossible, they cannot err. Nobody can be defeated and nobody can be victorious.

*Yagyu Tajima no Kami Munenori was a teacher of swordsmanship
to the shogun.
One of the personal guards of the shogun came to Tajima no Kami
one day asking to be trained in swordplay.
"As I observe, you seem to be a master of the art yourself," said the
teacher.*

"*As I observe ...* " said the master. In India, when Buddha was alive, one of his contemporaries was Mahavira. Between the disciples of the two there has been a great discussion ever since. The discussion is about an enlightened person's awareness. Mahavira's followers, the Jainas, say that whenever a person has become enlightened, he always knows everything of the past, of the present, of the future. He has become omniscient, he knows everything. He has become a mirror to the whole of the reality.

Buddha's followers say that that is not so. They say that he becomes capable of knowing anything if he observes. If he tries to focus on anything, he will be able to know everything about it. But it does not happen as the followers of Mahavira say, that whether he focuses or not he knows.

To me also, the Buddhist standpoint seems to be better and more scientific. Otherwise a man like Buddha would go almost mad. Just think of it: knowing everything of the past and the present and the future. No, that doesn't seem to be right. The Buddhist attitude seems to be more right: he has become *capable* of knowing. Now, whenever he wants to use the capacity, he focuses, he throws his ray of light. He puts something in the flow of his meditation and that thing becomes revealed to him. Otherwise it would be impossible for him to rest. Even in the night he would be continuously knowing, knowing the past and the present and the future – and not only his own, but of the whole world. Just think of the sheer impossibility of it. No, that's not possible.

"*As I observe ...* " said the master. The disciple has come and he has asked to be trained in swordplay. The master said, "*As I observe ...* " He focuses his ray of light, his torch, towards this disciple. Now this disciple is under his meditation. He goes through and through, the disciple becomes transparent. That is what happens when you come to a master: simply his light penetrates you to your very core.

" *... you seem to be a master of the art yourself," said the master.*

He could not find anything wrong in this man. Everything was as it should be, in tune, humming. This man was a beautiful song, he had already achieved.

*"Please tell me to what school you belong before we enter into the
relationship of teacher and pupil."*

That is the highest relationship in the world, greater than a love-relationship, greater than *any* relationship – because the surrender has to be total. Even in a love relationship it is not total: surrender is partial, a divorce is possible. But in fact, if you have once become a disciple of a master – if you have really become a disciple, if you have been accepted, if you have surrendered – there is no possibility of divorce, there is no going back. It is a point of no return. Then the two persons are no longer there. They exist like one, two aspects of one, but they are not two.

So the master says, "Before we enter into the relationship of teacher and pupil, I would like to know where you learned this art. How have you become so tuned? You are already a master."

The guardsman said, "I do not belong to any school, I have never studied the art."
"It is no use trying to fool me," said the master. "My judging eye never fails."

Now listen to this paradox: the judging eye arises only when you have left all judgment. In meditation you have to leave all judging: what is good, what is bad – you have to drop all that division. You simply look. You look without any judgment, without any condemnation, without any appreciation. You don't evaluate, you simply look. The look becomes pure.

When this look has happened to you and has become an integrated thing in your being, you attain to a capacity which never fails. Once you have become one inside and gone beyond morality, dualism – good and bad, sin and virtue, life and death, beautiful and ugly – once you have gone beyond the dualisms of mind you attain to the judging eye.

This is the paradox: all judgment has to be left, then you attain to the judging eye. Then it never fails. You simply know it is so and there is no alternative to it. It is not a choice on your part, it is not a decision. It is a simple revelation that it is so.

"It is no use trying to fool me," said the master. "My judging eye never fails."
"I am sorry to defy, your honor," said the guard, "but I really know nothing."
"If you say so, then it must be true, but I am sure you are the master of something ... "

Now this point has to be understood: it makes no difference what you are a master of, the taste of mastery is the same, the flavor is the same. You can become a master of archery, or you can become a master of swords-manship, or you can become a master just of the ordinary tea ceremony – it makes no difference. The real thing is that you have become a master. The art has gone so deep that you are not carrying it anymore. The art has gone so deep that now there is no need to think about it, it has become simply your nature.

" ... *but I am sure that you must be a master of something* ... " Maybe you are not a master of swordsmanship, but you are a master ...

" ... so tell me about yourself."
"There is one thing," said the guard. "When I was a child I thought
that a samurai, a warrior, should never be afraid of death. So I
grappled with the problem, and now the thought of death has
ceased to worry me."

But that is what the whole of religion is all about! If death no longer bothers you, you have become a master. You have tasted something of the deathless, that is, of your innermost nature. You have known something of the eternal. To know the deathless is the whole business of life. Life is an opportunity to know the deathless " ... *and now the thought of death has ceased to worry me."*

"That's it!" exclaimed the master. "The ultimate secrets of
swordsmanship lie in being released from the thought of death. You
need no technical training, you are already a master."

... because when you are fighting with a sword, if you are afraid of death, thinking will continue.

Now let me tell you one basic truth: thinking is out of fear. All thinking is out of fear. The more you become afraid, the more you think. Whenever there is no fear, thinking stops. If you have fallen in love with someone, there are moments with your beloved or your lover when thinking stops. Just sitting by the lake, doing nothing, holding hands, looking at the moon or the stars, or just gazing into the darkness of the night, sometimes thoughts stop because there is no fear. Love dispels fear just as light dispels darkness.

If even for a moment you have been in love with someone, fear disappears and thinking stops. With fear, thinking continues. The more you are afraid, the more you have to think – because by thinking you will create security, by thinking you will create a citadel around you, by thinking you will manage, or try to manage, how to fight.

A swordsman, if he is afraid of death, cannot be a real swordsman because the fear will make him tremble. A slight trembling inside, a slight thinking inside, and he will not be able to act out of no-mind.

There is a story:

A man in China became the greatest archer. He asked the king, "Declare me as the greatest archer of the country."

The king was just going to decide and declare him when an old servant of the king said, "Wait, sir. I know a man who lives in the forest, who never comes to the town. He is a greater archer. So let this young man go to him and learn from him for at least three years. He does not know what he is demanding. He is like a camel who has not yet come across a mountain. Archers don't live in the capitals, the real archers are in the mountains. I know one, and I know for certain that this other man is nothing."

Of course, this man was sent. He went. He could not believe that there could be a greater archer than he was, but he found the old man – and he was!

For three years he learned from him. Then one day, when he had learned everything, the thought arose in him that, "If I kill this old man, then I will be the greatest archer."

The old man had gone to cut wood and he was coming back carrying wood on his head. The young man hid behind a tree, waiting to kill him. He shot an arrow. The old man took a small piece of wood and threw it. It struck the arrow and the arrow turned back and wounded the young man very deeply.

The old man came, took out the arrow and said, "I knew this. I knew that some day or other you were going to do this. That's why I have not taught you this secret. Only one secret I have kept for myself. There is no need to kill me, I am not a competitor. But one thing I must tell you: my master is still alive, and I am nothing before him. You will have to go deeper into the mountains. He is a man of one hundred and twenty years, very old, but while he is alive nobody can pretend and nobody should even think of declaring themselves the greatest archer. You must be with him for at least thirty years – and he is very old, so go fast! Find the old man!"

The young man traveled, now very desperate. It seemed to be impossible to become the greatest archer in the country. He found the old man. He was so ancient – one hundred and twenty years old, completely bent – that he could not stand upright. But the young man was surprised because there was no bow, no arrows with him.

He asked, "Are you the old man who is the greatest archer?"

The old man said, "Yes."

"But where are your bow and arrows?"

The old man said, "Those are playthings. Real archers don't need them once they have learned the art. They are just devices to learn; once you have learned, you throw them away. A great musician will throw away his instrument because he has learned what music is. Then, carrying the instrument is foolish, childish. But if you are really interested in becoming an archer," said the old man, "then come with me."

He took him to a precipice. There was a rock overlooking a very deep valley. The old man went ahead of the young man and stood just at the very edge. With the slightest trembling he would topple down into the valley. He called the young man to come close to him.

The young man started perspiring, started trembling. It was so dangerous to be there. At just two feet away he said, "I cannot come that close."

The old man started laughing and he said, "If you tremble so much with fear, how can you become an archer? Fear must disappear totally, with no trace left behind."

The young man said, "But how can it be? I am afraid of death."

The old man said, "Drop the idea of death. Find someone who can teach you what a deathless life is and you will become the greatest archer, never before."

Fear creates trembling. Fear creates thinking. Thinking is a sort of inner trembling. When one becomes unwavering, the flame of consciousness remains there, undistracted, untrembling.

"That's it!" exclaimed the master. "The ultimate secrets of swordsmanship lie in being released from the thought of death. You need no technical training, you are already a master."

But he was not aware of his own mastery. He may have been hiding many other things, and because of that he was also hiding his treasures. Once exposed to a master, he became alert. And the master said, "There is no need for any techniques; you are already a master."

As I see in you, everybody is carrying deathlessness within him. You may know it, you may not know it — that is not the point — but you are carrying it within you. It is already there, it is already the case. Just a slight understanding of it and your life can be transformed. Then there is no need for any techniques.

Religion is not technology.

Everybody is born with a secret treasure but goes on living as if he were born a beggar. Everybody is born an emperor but goes on living like a beggar. Realize it! And the realization will come to you only if, by and by, you drop your fear.

So whenever fear comes to you don't suppress it, don't repress it, don't avoid it, don't get occupied in something so that you can forget about it. No! When fear comes, watch it. Be face to face with it. Encounter it. Look deeply into it. Gaze into the valley of fear. Of course you will perspire and you will tremble and it will be like a death – and you will have to live it many times. But by and by, the more your eyes become clear, the more your awareness becomes alert, the more your focus is there on the fear, the fear will disappear like a mist.

And once fear disappears, sometimes, even for only a moment, suddenly you are deathless.

There is no death. Death is the greatest illusion there is, the greatest myth, a lie. For even a single moment, if you can see that you are deathless, then no meditation is needed. Then live that experience. Then act out of that experience and the doors of eternal life are open for you.

Much is being missed because of fear. We are too attached to the body and we go on creating more and more fear because of that attachment. The body is going to die. The body is part of death, the body *is* death. But you are beyond the body. You are not the body, you are the bodiless. Remember it, realize it. Awaken yourself to this truth that you are beyond the body. You are the witness, the seer. Then death disappears, fear disappears, and there arises the tremendously glorious life, what Jesus calls 'life abundant, the kingdom of God'.

The kingdom of God is within you.

Enough for today.

Chapter 6

Madmen and Devotees

? **What's the difference between a madman and a devotee?**

Not much, and yet, much. Both are mad, but their madness has a totally different quality to it. The center of madness is different. The madman is mad from the head, the devotee is mad from the heart.

The madman is mad because of a failure. His logic failed; he could not go on with the head anymore, any longer. There comes a point for the logical mind where breakdown is a must because logic goes well up to a certain limit, then suddenly it is no longer real. Then it is no longer true to reality.

Life is illogical. It is wild. In life, contradictions are not contradictions but complementaries. Life does not believe in the division of either–or, life believes in both. The day becomes night, the night becomes day. They meet and merge, boundaries are not clear. Everything is overlapping everything else: you are overlapping into your beloved, your beloved is overlapping into you. Your child is still a part of you and yet he is independent – boundaries are blurred.

Logic makes clear-cut boundaries. For clarity, it dissects life into two, into a duality. Clarity is achieved, but aliveness is lost. At the cost of aliveness logic achieves clarity.

So if you are a mediocre mind, you may never go mad. That means you are just lukewarm, logical, and much that is illogical goes on existing in you side by side. But if you are really logical, then the ultimate result can only be madness. The more logical you are the more you will be intolerant of anything illogical. And life *is* illogical, so by and by you will become intolerant of life itself. You will become more and more closed. You will deny life, you will not deny logic. Then finally you break down. This is the failure of logic.

Almost all the great philosophers who are logical go mad. If they don't go mad they are not great philosophers. Nietzsche went mad, Bertrand Russell never went mad. He is not such a great philosopher; he is, in a way, mediocre. He goes on living with his common sense – he is a commonsensical philosopher. He does not move to the very extreme. Nietzsche moved to the very extreme and of course, then there is the abyss.

Madness is the failure of the head, and in life there are millions of situations where suddenly, the head is irrelevant.

I was reading an anecdote:

A woman telephoned the builder of her new house to complain about the vibrations that shook the structure when a train passed by three streets away.

"Ridiculous!" he told her. "I will be along to check it."

"Just wait until a train comes along," said the woman when the builder arrived for his inspection. "Why, it nearly shakes me out of bed. Just lie down there. You will see."

The builder had just stretched himself out on the bed when the woman's husband came home.

"What are you doing on my wife's bed?" the husband demanded.

The terrified builder shook like a leaf. "Would you believe I am waiting for a train?" he said.

There are a thousand and one situations where life comes in its total illogicalness. Suddenly your logical mind stops, it cannot function. If you watch life you will find you act illogically every day. And if you insist too much on logic then by and by you will get paralyzed; by and by you will be thrown away from life; by and by you will feel a certain deadness settling in you. One day or other this situation has to explode – the division of either – or breaks down.

Division, as such, is false. Nothing is divided in life. Only in your head is there division; only in your head are there clear-cut boundaries. It is as if you have made a small clearing in a forest – clean, with a boundary wall, with a lawn, with a few rosebushes, and everything perfectly in order. But beyond the boundary the forest is there, waiting. If you don't care about your garden for a few days, the forest will enter in. If you leave your garden untended, after a while the garden will disappear and the forest will be there. Logic is manmade, like an English garden – not even like a Zen Japanese garden, clean-cut.

Every day there is a difficulty. Mukta looks after my garden. She is my gardener, and she goes on cutting. I go on telling her, "Don't cut! Let it be like a forest!" But what can she do? She hides from me that she is cutting and planning and managing because she cannot allow the garden to become a forest. It should be in boundaries.

The logical mind is like a small garden, manmade, and life is wild forest. Sooner or later you will come against life and then your mind will boggle, will fall down flat. Stretch your mind to the very extreme of logic and you will go mad.

It happened at an airport: Moskowitz met his business rival, Levinson, at the airport, and asked him with an elaborate pretense of casualness, "And where do you happen to be going, Levinson?"

Levinson just as casually responded, "Chicago."

"Ah!" said Moskowitz, shaking his finger triumphantly. "Now I have caught you in a flatfooted lie. You tell me Chicago because you want me to think you are going to St. Louis, but I talked to your partner only this morning, and I happen to know you are going to Chicago, you liar!"

The logical mind goes on weaving and spinning its own theories, its own ideas, and tries to make the reality fit accordingly. The reality should follow your idea; that is what a logical mind is. The effort is that the reality should be a shadow to your ideology. But it is not possible, you are trying the impossible. It is implausible, it cannot happen. Ideology has to follow reality, and when the situation comes where you have to follow reality, the whole structure of your mind staggers, the whole structure of your mind simply drops down. It proves to be a house of playing cards: a small wind of reality and the palace disappears. That is madness.

What is the madness of a devotee? The center of the devotee's madness is his heart, the center of ordinary madness is the head. Ordinary madness happens from the failure of the head and the devotee's madness happens from the success of his heart, when love succeeds. When logic fails, ordinary madness; extraordinary madness, the madness of a devotee.

Love is illogical. Love is irrational. Love is life. Love comprehends all contradictions in it. Love is even capable of comprehending its own opposite: hate. Have you not observed it? You go on hating the same person you love. But love is bigger. It is so big that even hate can be allowed to have its play. In fact, if you really love, hate is not a distraction; on the contrary, it gives color, spice. It makes the whole affair more colorful, like a rainbow. Even hate is not the opposite for a loving heart: he can hate and continue loving. Love is so great that even hate can be allowed to have its own say. Lovers become intimate enemies, they go on fighting.

In fact, if you ask psychoanalysts, psychiatrists and psychologists, they will say that when a couple stop fighting, love has also stopped. When a couple no longer bother even to fight, have become indifferent to each other, then love has stopped. If you are still fighting with your wife or your husband, your boyfriend or girlfriend, that simply shows that life is still running in it. It is still a live wire – still hot. When love is no longer there and everything is dead, then there is no fight. Of course! What to fight for? It is meaningless. One settles into a sort of coldness; one settles into a sort of indifference.

Love is like wild life, hence Jesus' saying that God is love. What does he mean? He means that if you love you will know many things which are qualities of God: that he comprehends opposites, that even the Devil is allowed to have his say, that there is no problem with the opposite, that the enemy is also a friend and deep down related and connected, that death is not against life, but that death is part of life and life is part of death.

The whole is bigger than all opposites. And it is not just a total of all the opposites, it is more than the total. This is the higher mathematics of the heart. Of course a man of love will look mad. He will look mad to you because you function from the head and he functions from the heart; the languages are totally different.

For example, Jesus was crucified. The enemies were waiting for him to curse them, and they were a little afraid. The friends were waiting for him to do some miracle, that all the enemies would fall dead. And what did he do? He did an almost mad thing: he prayed to God to forgive these people because they didn't know what they were doing.

This is the madness of love. It is unexpected that when you are being killed you pray that these people should be forgiven because they don't know what they are doing. They are completely unconscious, sleepwalkers; whatsoever they are doing is not their responsibility because how can you throw responsibility on somebody who is asleep? "They are unconscious, forgive them." This is the miracle that happened that day, but nobody could see that miracle – it was sheer madness.

Love's language is so foreign to the head. Head and heart are the farthest poles of reality. There is no greater distance between any other two points than there is between the head and the heart, reason and love, logic and life.

If a person is mad because of his love, his madness is not a disease. In fact, he is the only healthy person. He is the only whole person; he is the only holy person because through his heart he has again become bridged with life. Now he is no longer fighting, there is no more conflict. He is surrendered, he is in a let-go. He trusts life. He has faith and he knows that nothing wrong is going to happen. He's not afraid. Even into death he will go laughing and singing, ecstatic, because even in death God is waiting for him, death also becomes a door.

Of course, to the logical mind, this man looks mad. And he is mad, in a sense, because whatsoever he is doing is beyond the comprehension of reason. But to me he is not mad. Ask Jesus: to him he is not mad. Ask Buddha: to him he is not mad, in fact he's the only sane person, because now he no longer thinks, he lives; now he is no longer divided, but total; now there is no duality in him, he is a unity.

That is the meaning of the word *yoga*: that which unites. That is the meaning of the word *religion* also: that which makes you one, that which puts you together again, *religere*; you are no longer split.

Otherwise, ordinarily you are not one person, you are many persons. You are a crowd. You don't know what your left hand is doing and what your right hand is planning to do. In the morning you don't know what you are going to do in the evening. You say one thing but you wanted say something else, and you will go on saying something else still. You are not a unity, you are a crowd. There are many persons inside you revolving in a wheel and each becomes, for the time being, the king. And in that moment the king asserts things which he cannot fulfill, because by the time the moment to fulfill them comes, he will no longer be a king.

You fall in love with a woman and you say, "I will love you forever and forever." Wait! What are you saying? Now, at this moment, a certain part of your personality is on the throne and that part says, "I will love you forever and forever," but just half an hour later you may repent. And just a few days later you will completely forget what you had said.

The woman is not going to forget it, she will remember. She will remind you again and again about what you have said, that you will love her forever and forever. What has happened to your love? You will feel guilty and you will feel impotent and helpless because you cannot do anything. Now you know you should not have talked about the future, but at that moment you could not resist yourself; at that moment it looked as if you would be loving her forever and forever. In that moment it was a truth, but the part of the mind that asserted it is no longer the emperor. Now there are other minds: another part is sitting on the throne and he loves another woman, he chooses another woman. Whatsoever you promise, you are not going to fulfill.

A man of understanding never promises because he knows his helplessness. He will say, "I would like to love you forever and forever, but who knows? I may not be the same the next day." He will feel humble, he will not feel confident. Only fools feel confident. People of understanding hesitate because they know there is a crowd inside them, they are not one.

That's why in all the old scriptures it is said that if a good thought comes to you do it immediately, because the next moment you may not like to do it at all. And if a bad thought comes to you postpone it a little. If anything good arises in you don't miss the moment, do it! If you feel it is good you can do it again tomorrow, but do it right now, don't postpone.

But the ordinary mind goes on doing just the opposite: whatsoever good arises in you, you postpone it for tomorrow – then it never happens – and whatsoever bad arises in you, you do it immediately. If you are angry you will be angry right now, you cannot postpone it. But if you are feeling compassion you will say, "What is the hurry? Tomorrow!" That tomorrow never comes. Tomorrow is non-existential.

Ordinarily, a man is a crowd. In fact, we should not use the word *mind* in singular. We should not say that you have a mind. That is wrong. Only rare persons have a mind. You have minds. You are poly-psychic.

The heart – this is the beautiful thing – the heart is always one. It does not know the duality. It is not a crowd, it is a unity. The closer you come to the heart, "the one" arises and "the many" disappears far away. The heart needs no promise – even without promising it is going to fulfill.

The mind goes on making promises but it never fulfills them. In fact, it promises just to create an illusion because it knows it is not going to fulfill anything. So at least create an illusion by promising, "I will love you for ever and ever." The heart will never say that, but it will do it. And when you can do it what is the point of saying it? There is no need.

The man of love is mad, mad to the logical mind, but he is not ill. In the Western madhouses there are many people who are not mad. If they had been in Eastern countries they may even have been worshipped. In the West this clarity does not yet exist that a man can be head-oriented mad or heart-oriented mad. A heart-oriented madman is not a madman, he is a godly man; or he is mad in such a different way that he needs to be worshipped, revered, respected. There is no need to treat him, there is no need to put him in an asylum, there is no need to give him shocks. But things go to the extreme, always.

In the East it has happened that many mad people have been worshipped – those who were mad from the head. They were simply crazy but they were worshipped because we have worshipped the madman of the heart, and it is very difficult for the ordinary, common masses to make the distinction – they look almost alike.

Now in the West the opposite is happening: people who would have been saints in the past. Just think, if Jesus came, was born in America today, where would he be? Or Saint Francis of Assisi – where would he be? In some madhouse. Jews treated Jesus very well: they killed him but they never put him in a madhouse. That was more respectful.

But now, in the modern world, if he came back to somewhere in the West, he would be in a madhouse, or lying down on some Freudian couch or being given some electric shocks, drugged – because psychoanalysts say that he was neurotic, his personality was neurotic, he was mad. Of course the things that he said looked mad. He said, "I am the son of God." What nonsense! Son of God? – megalomania! What is he talking about? He is not in his senses, he lives in a dream. He talks about the kingdom of God – all nonsense, fairy tales, good for children's books but immature. He chose a better time to come.

Saint Francis of Assisi would certainly be in a madhouse: talking to trees, saying to the almond tree, "Sister, how are you?" If he were here he would have been caught: "What are you doing? Talking to an almond tree?" "Sister, sing to me of God," he says to the almond tree. And not only that, he hears the song that the sister almond tree sings! Crazy! Needs treatment! He talks to the river and to the fish, and he claims that the fish respond to him. He talks to stones and rocks: is there any need for any more proof that he is mad?

He is mad, but wouldn't you like to be mad like Saint Francis of Assisi? Just think: the capacity to hear the almond tree singing and the heart that can feel brothers and sisters in trees, the heart that can talk to the rock, the heart that sees God everywhere, all around, in every form — it must be a heart of utmost love. Utter love reveals that mystery to you.

But for the logical mind, of course, these things are nonsense. To me, or to anybody who has known how to look at life through the heart, these are the only meaningful things. Become mad, if you can, become mad from the heart.

Now the last thing about this question: if your head comes to a breakdown, don't be worried. Use this opportunity of a destructured state. In that moment, don't be worried that you are going mad; in that moment, slip into the heart.

Someday in the future when psychology really comes of age, whenever somebody goes mad from the head we will help him to move towards the heart, because an opportunity opens in that moment. The breakdown can become a breakthrough. The old structure is gone, now he is no longer in the clutches of reason, he is free for a moment. Modern psychology tries to go on adjusting him back to the old structure. All modern efforts are about adjusting: how to make him normal again. Real psychology will do something else. Real psychology will use this opportunity — because the old mind has disappeared, there is a gap — use this interval and lead him towards another mind, that is, the heart. It will lead him towards another center of his being.

When you drive a car you change gears. Whenever you change the gear, there comes a moment when the gear moves through neutral; it has to move through the neutral gear. Neutral gear means no gear. From one gear to another, a moment comes when there is no gear. When one mind has failed, you are in a neutral state. Just now you are again as if you are born. Use this opportunity and lead the energy away from the old rotten structure which is falling. Leave the ruin, move into the heart. Forget reason and let love be your center, your target. Each breakdown can become a breakthrough. And each possibility for the failure of the head can become a success for the heart.

The failure of the head can become a success for the heart.

? **Once at darshan I heard you say of a visitor that he would be a good sannyasin. What is a good sannyasin?**

First, what is a sannyasin?

A sannyasin is one who has come to understand the futility of so-called worldly life. A sannyasin is one who has understood one thing: that something needs to be done immediately about his own being. If he goes on drifting in the old way, he will lose the whole opportunity of this life. A sannyasin is one who has become alert that up to now he has lived wrongly, has moved in wrong directions, has been too concerned with things and not concerned with himself, has been too concerned with worldly prestige and power and has not been concerned about who he is. A sannyasin is one who is turning towards himself, *paravritti*. A sannyasin is a miracle – the energy is moving back towards oneself.

Ordinarily the energy is moving away from you, towards things, targets, in the world. The energy is moving away from you, hence you feel empty. The energy goes away, never comes back; you go on throwing energy away. By and by you feel dissipated, frustrated; nothing comes back. By and by you start to feel empty; the energy is just oozing out every day. And then comes death. Death is nothing else but that you are exhausted and spent. The greatest miracle in life is to understand this and to turn the energy towards home. It is a turning in. This turning in, *paravritti*, is sannyas.

It is not that you leave the world. Live in the world, there is no need to leave anything or go anywhere else. Live in the world but in a totally different way: now you live in the world but you remain centered in yourself, your energy goes on returning to yourself.

You are no longer outgoing, you have become ingoing. Of course you become a pool of energy, a reservoir, and energy is delight, sheer delight. Just energy there, overflowing, and you are in delight and you can share and you can give in love. This is the difference. If you put your energy into greed it never comes back; if you put your energy into love it comes back a thousandfold. If you put your energy into anger it never comes back. It leaves you empty, exhausted, spent; if you use your energy in compassion it comes back a thousandfold.

So now I will tell you what a good sannyasin is. A good sannyasin is one who has understood this fundamental law of life: that giving love, it comes back a thousandfold. Give in anger and it is gone forever; give in greed and it is gone forever. Share it and it is never gone; on the contrary, you are enriched.

When I say "a good sannyasin" I don't mean a moral or immoral sannyasin: my word *good* has nothing to do with morality. It is something to do with what Buddha calls *ais dhammo sanantano*, what Buddha calls the eternal law of life.

A good man is an understanding man. A good man is alert, aware, that's all. Awareness is the only value for me, all else is meaningless. Awareness is the only value for me, so when I say "a good sannyasin," I mean a sannyasin who is aware. Of course when you are aware you behave according to the law, the fundamental law. When you are unaware you go on destroying yourself, you go on being suicidal.

If you behave according to the fundamental law you will be enriched tremendously. Your life will become richer and richer every moment. You will become a king. You may remain a beggar in the outside world, but you will become a king, a pinnacle of inner richness. What Jesus calls the kingdom of God is within you. You will become a king of the kingdom that is within you – but more awareness is needed.

So don't misunderstand me. When I say "a good sannyasin" I don't use the word in any moralistic sense. I use it in a more fundamental sense, because to me morality is just a byproduct of awareness, and immorality is a shadow of unawareness. I am not concerned with shadows and byproducts; I am concerned with the fundamental, with the essential.

Be aware and you will be good, be unaware and you will be bad.

I have heard a small anecdote:

An old farmer was watching his young son, Luke, lighting the wick of the hurricane lamp prior to departing for the evening.

"What is the lantern for?" he asked.

Said his son casually, "I am off courting, Dad. Don't worry, I will pay for the oil."

"Dang me!" said the father, "When I was a-courting, I never took me no lamp along, son."

"That figures," came the reply. "Look what you got!"

If you don't take the lamp of awareness with you, you are going to create a hell around you. Light your lamp wherever you go; courting, not courting, that is not the point. Wherever you go, whatsoever you do, always do it in the inner light, with awareness.

And don't be worried about moralities, concepts about what is good and what is bad. Good follows your inner light just like a shadow. Take care of the inner light.

That's what meditation is all about: to become more alert. Live the same life, just change your alertness, make it more intense. Eat the same food, walk the same path, live in the same house, be with the same woman and the children, but be totally different from your inside. Be alert! Walk the same path but with awareness. If you become aware, suddenly the path is no longer the same, because you are no longer the same. If you are aware, the same food is not the same because you are not the same, the same woman is not the same because you are not the same. Everything changes with your inner change.

If somebody changes his within, the without changes totally. My definition of the world is that you must be living in a deep inner darkness — hence the world. If you light your inner lamp, suddenly the world disappears and there is only godliness. The world and godliness are not two things but two perceptions of the same energy. If you are unaware the energy appears to you to be as the world, the *sansara*; if you are alert the same energy appears as godliness. The whole thing depends on your inner awareness or unawareness. That is the only change, the only transformation, the only revolution that has to be made.

❓ I feel sick with cowardice.

There must be a desire not to be a coward. That desire creates the problem. If you are a coward, you are a coward. Accept it. What can you do about it? Whatsoever you do will create more problems, more complexities.

And who is not a coward? When life is constantly in danger of death, how is it possible not to be a coward? It is impossible! When any moment you can die and life can be taken away from you, how is it possible, in the face of such danger, to be brave? You can pretend, you can manage to show that you are brave, but deep down you are going to remain a coward. It is natural. Just look at the tininess of human beings — so tiny, and existence is so vast. We are not even like drops, fighting against such an ocean. How is it possible not to be a coward?

Try to understand it. Accept it, it is natural. Don't create a goal against it because that goal is coming out of your cowardice. That goal is not going to help you. At the most you can become very tense and pretend that you are not a coward. You can move to the opposite extreme just to prove to the world and to yourself that you are not a coward.

That's what your generals and your great leaders are doing, just trying to prove to the world that they are not cowards. And because of their efforts the whole world has suffered tremendously. Please, don't try any foolish thing like that. Just accept. It is helplessness. One has to accept it. Once you accept it and you start understanding it, you will see that by and by it disappears. Not that you become brave — but one day you simply find that through acceptance it disappears.

There is no fight, it disappears. There is no resistance; you accept it and it disappears. It is not that you become brave, you simply become more understanding. Bravery is not a goal.

But you have been taught from your very childhood, "Be brave!" so you go on trying to be brave. That creates much anxiety and tension. You are trembling everywhere inside and on the outside you are like a stone statue, divided. This has created much misery in you.

The goals that have been taught to you from your childhood are foolish, are simply not based on reality. It is as if you say to a small leaf on a tree, "When strong winds come, don't shake, don't waver, don't tremble. That is cowardice." But what can a small leaf do? When the strong wind comes it shakes, the whole tree shakes. But trees are not so foolish, they won't listen to you, they go on doing their thing.

Have you watched two dogs fighting? They don't start fighting immediately. First they move in a mock fight. Both start barking. That is just a game to gauge, to judge, who is the stronger. They are not going to fight immediately because that is foolish, stupid; that is done only by human beings. First they will try to bark at each other, jump at each other, show their totality. The one will show "I am this" and the other will show "I am this." Then immediately they judge: that judgment needs nobody else to convince them. Immediately one feels that he is weaker, he puts his tail down and moves: "This is finished. What is the point of fighting? I am weaker and you are stronger and the stronger is going to win! The point is lost." It is not that he is a coward; he is simply wise. I don't call this cowardice.

Human beings will stay even if you feel that you are weak. The more you feel that you are weak, the more you will be afraid to leave. People will say you are a coward, so you must fight, and you will be beaten badly and unnecessarily hurt.

There is no point. It is a simple calculation. And the stronger one doesn't go and show the other dogs that he has won. No, the thing is simply dropped. He also knows that he is stronger, so what is the point? He doesn't go on advertising that he has won. No, the fight is dropped, he forgets all about it.

But in the human situation the whole thing has taken a very wrong shape, because you have been taught wrong goals. Each child should be taught to be true to life. If there is fear, then be afraid. Why hide it? Why pretend that you are not afraid? If you want to cry, cry. Why be afraid of tears? But we have been taught not to cry, particularly men. With small children the mother will say, "Don't be a sissy. Don't start crying, that is only for girls." And the boy becomes hard. Look. Men cannot cry. They have missed one of the most beautiful things in life. Nature has not made any difference between man and woman. Man has as many tear glands as woman, so the thing is proved, there is no difference. Tears are needed. They are cleansing. But how to cry? What will people say? They will say, "You, and crying? Your wife has died and you are crying? Be a man. Be brave, face it. Don't cry."

But do you understand? If you don't cry, by and by your smile will be corrupted, because everything is joined together. If you cannot cry you cannot laugh. If you don't allow your tears to flow naturally you will not be able to allow your smiles also to flow naturally. Everything will become unnatural, everything will become strained. Everything will become a forced thing and you will move almost in a diseased way and you will never be at ease with yourself. That is what has happened, and now you are miserable.

Life consists of flowing. If you are a coward, be a coward. Be honestly a coward. And I tell you there is nobody else who is not a coward. And it is good that people are not that way; otherwise even while they are so helpless, they would feel so egoistic. If they were not cowards they would be almost dead stones, they would not be alive — just egos, frozen.

Don't be bothered — accept it. If it is there, it is there, a fact of life. Try to understand it. Don't listen to others; you are still being manipulated by others.

I was reading an anecdote:

Mrs. Jones pursued her small husband through the crowds at the zoo brandishing her umbrella and emitting cries of menace. The frightened Mr. Jones, noticing the lock on the lions' cage had not quite caught, wrenched it off, flew into the cage, slammed the door shut again, pushed the astonished lion hard against the door and peered over its shoulder.

His frustrated wife shook her umbrella at him and yelled furiously, "Come out of there, you coward!"

This man, a coward?

But each husband is a coward in the eyes of the wife. In others' eyes, you are a coward. Don't trust the opinion of others too much. If you feel yourself to be a coward, close your eyes, meditate on it. Ninety-nine percent is others' opinion: the wife brandishing her umbrella, "Come out, you coward!" Ninety-nine percent is others' opinion, drop it; one percent is reality, accept it; and don't create any antagonistic goal. Accept it and then you will see that cowardice is no longer cowardice. Rejected, it becomes cowardice. The very word *cowardice* is a condemnation. Accepted, it becomes humbleness, helplessness.

That's how it is. We have to be humble: we are not the whole. We are the parts of a tremendously vast whole, very tiny parts, atomic parts, small leaves on a big tree.

It is good to tremble sometimes, nothing wrong in it. It helps you to shake off the dust. You become fresh again.

My whole point is, accept life as it is and don't try to change it into something else. Don't try to change your violence into nonviolence; don't try to change your cowardice into bravery; don't try to change your sex into celibacy. Don't create the opposite. Rather, try to understand the fact of violence, and by and by you will become nonviolent. Understand the fact of cowardice and cowardice will disappear. Understand the fact of sex and you will find a new quality arising in it which goes beyond it. But always move through the fact, never against it.

? My father is obsessed with genealogy. Is there anything to such pursuits?

Must be, otherwise why should your father be obsessed? He may have taken a wrong route, but there must be something in it. Even when people go astray they go astray for a certain reason, although they may not be aware of it.

For example, let me tell you an anecdote first:

Young Willie, aged eight, came to his father one morning and said, "Daddy, where did I come from?"

Willie's father felt a sinking sensation in his stomach, for he knew he was now up against it. He was a modern parent and realized a question like that deserved a full and frank answer. He found a quiet spot, and for the next half hour he carefully indoctrinated Willie into what are euphemistically called "the facts of life," managing to be quite explicit.

Willie listened with fascinated absorption, and when it was over, the father said, "Well, Willie, does that answer your question?"

"No," said Willie, "it does not. Johnny Brown came from Cincinnati, where did I come from?"

If your father is interested in genealogy he has misunderstood his inquiry. This is a natural question in everybody's being: from where do we come? From where, from what source? Now if you get into genealogy, you are not getting anywhere. The basic question is religious, it has nothing to do with genealogy. The basic question is: who is the ultimate father or ultimate mother?" The basic question is: where is the beginning of all?

Now this is pointless. I have a father, and my father had a father, and of course this goes on and on and you can go on searching and you can make a big tree of your family, but it is pointless because the question remains the same: who is the first?

Searching into genealogy, you cannot come to the first. Always the question will remain, "From whom?" I can move a hundred generations back or a thousand generations back, but the question remains the same, it is not solved: from where? From where, from what source, has life arisen?

Your father has missed. He has misinterpreted a religious inquiry. He has been thinking that it is a question of genealogy. It is not.

This question, "From where do I come?" has to be asked because unless I know that, it is impossible to know who I am.

There are two ways to know it. Either you ask, "From where do I come?" That is the way of the Christian, the Mohammedan and the Judaic religion. If you know from where you come, what the ultimate source is, what God is, then you will know who you are.

Indian religions have a different way of solving it, and a better and more scientific way. Hinduism, Jainism, Buddhism say it is difficult to know from where you come. There is more of a possibility that you may be lost in thinking and in philosophical doctrines. The better question is: Who am I? If you know this, you will know from where you come. So they say to forget all about God. They are not worried about who created the world, they are worried about, "Who am I?"

In a way that is more scientific, because if I can understand the quality of my being, that will immediately give me the key to understanding the whole and what it is. If I can understand myself — because the source must still be existing in some way within me. The tree still goes on existing in the seed: if you can understand the seed you will be able to know the tree; in the fruit, the whole tree exists.

If we can understand ourselves ... Of course this is the closest approach possible, because I am closer to myself than anything else. Just close your eyes and you reach into yourself. The only problem is how to drop the thoughts. Then, suddenly, you start sinking into your being. From there is the door to the whole, to the source.

When you go back home, tell your father that genealogy is not going to help. He must have some religious inquiry within him which he has misunderstood. Once he is made aware of it his inquiry will be on the right lines.

It is happening in the West because religion is no longer an accepted inquiry, it is a rejected inquiry, so people go on seeking religious inquiries through vicarious ways. You cannot accept directly that you are seeking God; people will think you are mad! "It is foolish. What are you talking about? Then you are not a contemporary. God is dead, have you not heard? What are you doing?" But the desire arises to know the source, and you cannot accept it in religious ways because religious ways are no longer accepted by the modern mind. So you have to search for it in a vicarious way — then you start asking about genealogy.

Religion is a valid inquiry. It doesn't matter whether society accepts it or rejects it. Man is a religious animal and is going to remain that way. Religion is something natural. To ask from where you come is relevant; to ask, "Who am I?" is always going to remain relevant. But the modern mind has created a climate of atheism so you cannot ask such questions. If you ask, people laugh. If you talk about such things, people feel bored. If you start inquiring in these ways, people think you are slipping out of your sanity. Religion is no longer a welcome inquiry.

Tell your father. And of course, genealogy will remain an obsession because this is not the right inquiry, but once his consciousness shifts to the religious dimension he will be released from the obsession. And then something is possible, something of tremendous import is possible. He wants to know who the real father is, who has fathered existence, or who is still mothering existence.

The last question. Listen to it very carefully, it is very important.

> **How do you manage it, to have always the right anecdote at the right moment?**

Let me answer you with an anecdote:

A king, passing through a small town, saw what he took to be indications of amazing marksmanship. On trees, barns and fences there were numbers of bull's-eyes, each with a bullet hole in the exact center. He could not believe his eyes. It was superb marksmanship, almost a miracle of achievement. He himself was a good marksman, and he had known many great marksmen in his life, but never anything like this. He asked to meet the expert shot. It turned out to be a madman.

"This is sensational! How in the world do you do it?" he asked the madman. "I myself am a good shot, but nothing compared to your skill and art. Please tell me."

"Easy as pie!" said the madman and laughed uproariously. "I shoot first and draw the circles in later!"

Dig? I choose the anecdotes first and then draw the circles. I am just like that madman.

There are other people who use anecdotes to illustrate some theoretical point. I do just the opposite: I use theoretical points to illustrate the anecdotes.

Enough for today.

Chapter 7

The Proper State of Mind

When wolves were discovered in the village near Master Shoju's
temple, Shoju entered the graveyard nightly for one week and sat
in zazen. This put a stop to the wolves' prowling. Overjoyed, the
villagers asked him to describe the secret rites he had performed.
"I didn't have to resort to such things," he said, "nor could I have
done so. While I was in zazen a number of wolves gathered round
me, licking the tip of my nose and sniffing my windpipe, but because
I remained in the right state of mind, I wasn't bitten. As I keep
preaching to you, the proper state of mind will make it possible for
you to be free in life and death, invulnerable to fire and water. Even
wolves are powerless against it. I simply practice what I preach."

What is meditation? Is it a technique that can be practiced? Is it an effort that you have to do? Is it something which the mind can achieve? It is not.

All that the mind can do cannot be meditation. It is something beyond the mind; the mind is absolutely helpless there. The mind cannot penetrate meditation: where mind ends, meditation begins. This has to be remembered, because in our life, whatsoever we do, we do through the mind; whatsoever we achieve, we achieve through the mind. And then when we turn inward we again start thinking in terms of techniques, methods, doings, because the whole of life's experience shows us that everything can be done by the mind.

Yes, except meditation, everything can be done by the mind. Everything *is* done by the mind except meditation, because meditation is not an achievement. It is already the case, it is your nature. It has not to be achieved, it has only to be recognized, it has only to be remembered. It is there waiting for you – just a turning in and it is available. You have been carrying it always and always.

Meditation is your intrinsic nature. It is you, it is your being. It has nothing to do with your doings. You cannot have it. You cannot *not* have it. It cannot be possessed, it is not a thing. It is you, it is your being.

Once you understand what meditation is, things become very clear. Otherwise you can go on groping in the dark.

Meditation is a state of clarity, not a state of mind. Mind is confusion. Mind is never clear, it cannot be. Thoughts create clouds around you, they are subtle clouds. A mist is created by them and the clarity is lost. When thoughts disappear, when there are no more clouds around you, when you are in your simple being-ness, clarity happens. Then you can see far away, then you can see to the very end of existence. Then your gaze becomes penetrating, to the very core of being.

Meditation is clarity, absolute clarity of vision. You cannot think about it. You have to drop thinking. When I say you have to drop thinking, don't conclude in a hurry. Because I have to use language, so I say, "Drop thinking" – but if you start dropping you will miss, because again you will reduce it to a doing.

"Drop thinking" simply means don't do anything. Sit. Let thoughts settle themselves. Let mind drop on its own accord. Just sit gazing at the wall in a silent corner, not doing anything at all, relaxed, loose, with no effort, not going anywhere, as if you are falling asleep awake. You are awake and you are relaxing and the whole body is falling into sleep. You remain alert inside and the whole body moves into deep relaxation.

Thoughts settle on their own accord. You need not jump amongst them, you need not try to put them right. It is as if a stream has become muddy: what do you do? Do you jump in it and start helping the stream to become clear? – you will make it more muddy.

You simply sit on the bank. You wait. There is nothing to be done, because whatsoever you do will make the stream more muddy. If somebody has passed through the stream and the dead leaves have surfaced, the mud has arisen, just patience is needed. You simply sit on the bank. Watch indifferently: the stream goes on flowing, the dead leaves will be taken away – and the mud cannot be there forever, it will start settling. After a while, suddenly you will become aware the stream is crystal-clear again.

Whenever a desire passes through your mind, the stream becomes muddy. Just sit. Don't try to do anything. In Japan this "just sitting" is called zazen – just sitting and doing nothing. And one day meditation happens. Not that you bring it to you, it comes to you. And when it comes, you immediately recognize it. It has always been there but you were not looking in the right direction. The treasure has been with you but you were occupied somewhere else: in thoughts, in desires, in a thousand and one things. You were not interested in only one thing – and that was your own being.

When energy turns in – what Buddha calls *paravritti*, the coming back of your energy to the source – suddenly clarity is attained. Then you can see clouds a thousand miles away, and then you can hear ancient music in the pines. Then everything is available to you.

Before we enter this beautiful Zen story a few things about the mind have to be understood, because the more you understand the mechanism of the mind, the more is the possibility that you will not interfere. The more you understand how the mind functions, the more is the possibility that you will be able to sit in zazen, that you will be able just to sit – sitting and doing nothing – that you will be able to allow meditation to happen. It is a happening.

But the understanding of the mind will be helpful. Otherwise you may go on doing something which helps the mind to function, which goes on giving cooperation to the mind.

The first thing about the mind is that it is a constant chattering. Whether you are talking or not, it goes on doing some inner talk; whether you are awake or asleep the inner talk continues as an undercurrent. You may be doing some work but the inner talk continues. You are driving, or you are digging a hole in the garden, but the inner talk continues.

The mind is constantly talking. If the inner talk can drop even for a single moment you will be able to have a glimpse of no-mind. That's what meditation is all about. The state of no-mind is the right state; it is *your* state.

But how to come to an interval where the mind stops the inner chattering? If you try, again you will miss. But there is no need to try. In fact, the interval is continuously happening. Just a little alertness is needed. Between two thoughts there is an interval; even between two words there is a gap. Otherwise words will run over each other, otherwise thoughts will overlap each other.

They don't overlap, whatsoever you say. You say, "A rose is a rose is a rose:" between two words there is a gap; between *a* and *rose* there is a gap, howsoever small, howsoever invisible, howsoever imperceptible. But the gap is there, otherwise *a* will run over *ros'*. With just a little alertness, just a little watchfulness and you can see the gap: *a ... rose ... is ... a ... rose ... is ... a ... rose*. The gap is continuously recurring; after each word the gap is recurring.

The gestalt has to be changed. Ordinarily you look at the words, you don't look at the gaps. You look at the *a*, you look at the *rose*, but you don't look at the gap between the two. Change your attention.

Have you seen children's books? There are many pictures, and you can look at the same picture in two ways: if you look one way there is an old woman, but if you go on looking, suddenly the picture changes and a young, beautiful woman can be seen. The same lines make both faces – of an old woman and a young woman. If you go on looking at the young face, again it changes because the mind cannot remain constant at anything; it is a flux. And if you go on looking again at the old face it will change back to a young face.

You will notice one thing: when you see the old face you cannot see the young face, though you know it is hidden somewhere, you have known it, you have seen it. And when you see the young face, the old face cannot be seen. It disappears although you know it is there. But you cannot see both together; they are contradictory. They cannot be seen together: when you see the figure the background disappears, when you see the background the figure disappears.

Mind has a limited capacity to know; it cannot know the contradictory. That's why it cannot know godliness: godliness is contradictory. That's why it cannot know the innermost core of your being: it is contradictory. It comprehends all contradictions, it is paradoxical.

The mind can see only one thing at a time, and the opposite is not possible at the same time. When you see the opposite, the first disappears. The mind goes on looking at the words so it cannot see the silences that come after each word.

Change the focus. Just sitting silently, start looking in the gaps – not with effort, no need to strain; relaxed, just easy, in a playful mood, just as a fun. No need to be religious about it, otherwise you become serious. And once you become serious it is very difficult to move from words to no words. It is very easy if you remain loose, flowing, non-serious, playful – as if it is just a fun.

Millions of people miss meditation because meditation has taken on a wrong connotation. It looks very serious, looks gloomy, has something of the church in it; looks as if it is only for people who are either dead, or almost dead, who are gloomy, serious, have long faces; who have lost festivity, fun, playfulness, celebration. These are the qualities of meditation. A really meditative person is playful, life is fun for him. Life is a *leela*, a play. He enjoys it tremendously. He is not serious, he is relaxed.

Sit silently, relaxed, loose. Just allow your attention to flow towards the gaps. Slip from the edges of words into the intervals. Let intervals become more prominent and allow words to fade away. It is just as if you are looking at a blackboard and I put a small white dot on it: you can see either the dot, then the blackboard goes far away, or you can see the blackboard, then the dot becomes secondary, a shadow phenomenon. You can go on changing your attention between the figure and the background.

Words are figures, silence is the background. Words come and go, silence remains. When you were born you were born as a silence – just intervals and intervals, gaps and gaps. You came with infinite emptiness, you brought unbounded emptiness with you in life. Then you started collecting words.

That's why if you go back in your memory, if you try to remember, you cannot go past the age of four. Because before the age of four you were almost empty. Words started collecting in your memory after the age of four. Memory can function only where words function. Emptiness leaves no trace on you. That's why when you go back and you try to remember, you can remember, at the most, the age of four, or if you were very intelligent then your remembering can go back to the age of three. But there comes a point where suddenly there is no memory.

Up to that time you were an emptiness – pure, virgin, uncorrupted by words. You were pure sky. The day you die, again your words will drop and scatter. You will move into another world or another life again with your emptiness.

Emptiness is your self.

I have heard that Shankara used to tell the story of a pupil who kept asking his master about the nature of the ultimate self. Each time the question came, the master would turn a deaf ear – until finally he turned on his pupil one day and said, "I am teaching you, but you do not follow. The self is silence."

Mind means words, *self* means silence. Mind is nothing but all the words that you have accumulated. Silence is that which has always been with you, it is not an accumulation. That is the meaning of self: it is your intrinsic quality. On the background of silence you go on accumulating words, and the words in total are known as "the mind." Silence is meditation. It is a question of changing the gestalt, shifting the attention from words into silence – which is always there.

Each word is like a precipice: you can take a jump into the valley of silence. From each word you can slip into silence. That is the use of a mantra. *Mantra* means repeating a single word again and again and again. When you repeat a single word again and again and again, you get bored with that word because the novelty is lost. You get fed up with that word, you want to get rid of that word. Boredom helps, it helps you to get rid of the word – now you can slip more easily into silence.

The silence is always there round the corner. If you go on repeating *Ram, Ram, Ram* ... How long can you repeat it? Sooner or later you feel fed up, bored. The use of a mantra is to create such boredom that you want to get rid of it. That state is beautiful, because then there is no other way than to slip into silence. Leave the word behind and move into the gap; use the word as a jumping board and jump into the abyss.

If words change, as they always change ... Ordinarily, of course, you are never fed up. A new word is always attractive, a new idea is always attractive, a new dream, a new desire, is always attractive. But if you can see that the mind is simply repeating the same thing again and again and again: either you fall asleep or you jump into silence, these are the two possibilities. And I know that most people who chant mantras fall into sleep. That too is a possibility which we have known for centuries.

Mothers know it well. When a child is not falling asleep they do a mantra. They call it a lullaby. They repeat just two or three words in a monotonous tone and the child starts feeling sleepy. Go on repeating and the child gets bored – and he cannot escape, he cannot go anywhere, so the only escape is into sleep. He says, "Go on repeating. I am going to sleep!" and he falls asleep.

Many chanters of mantras fall asleep, hence the use of Transcendental Meditation for people who suffer from sleeplessness; hence its appeal in America. Insomnia has become a normal thing. The more insomnia there is, the more will be the appeal of Maharishi Mahesh Yogi because people need some tranquilizers. A mantra is a perfect tranquilizer, but that is not its real use. There is nothing wrong in it; if it gives you good sleep, good – but that is not its real use.

It is as if you are using an airplane like a bullock cart. You can use it, you can put the airplane behind bullocks and use it as a bullock car – nothing wrong in it, it will serve a little purpose, but that is not its use. You could soar very high with it.

A mantra has to be used with full awareness that this is to create boredom, and you are to remember not to fall asleep. Otherwise, you miss. Don't fall asleep. Go on repeating the mantra and don't allow yourself to fall into sleep. So it is better if you repeat the mantra standing, or repeat it walking, so that you don't fall asleep.

One of the great disciples of Gurdjieff, P.D. Ouspensky, was dying. The doctors told him to rest but he would not rest; instead he continued walking the whole night. They thought he had gone crazy. He was dying, his energy was disappearing – what was he doing? This was the time to rest; he would die sooner if he went on walking. But he would not stop.

Somebody asked, "What are you doing?"

He said, "I would like to die alert, awake. I don't want to die asleep, otherwise I will miss the beauty of death." And he died walking.

That is the way to do a mantra: walk.

If you go to Bodh Gaya where Gautama the Buddha attained enlightenment, near the bodhi tree you will find a small path. On that path Buddha walked continuously: for one hour he would meditate under the tree, and then for one hour he would walk.

When his disciples asked, "Why?" he would say, "Because if I sit too much under the tree, then sleepiness starts coming."

The moment sleepiness starts coming one has to walk because otherwise you will slip into sleep and the whole mantra is lost. The mantra is to create boredom, the mantra is to create a fed up-ness so that you can jump into the abyss. But if you move into sleep the abyss is missed.

All Buddhist meditations alternate: you do them sitting, but when you feel drowsiness setting in, immediately you get up and start doing them walking. Then the moment you see that the sleepiness has disappeared, sit again, do the meditation again. If you go on doing this, a moment comes when suddenly you slip out of the words, just like a snake who slips out of his old skin. And it happens very naturally, there is no effort to it.

So the first thing to remember about mind is: it is a constant chattering. That chattering keeps it alive, that chattering is a food for it. Without that chattering the mind cannot continue. So drop out of the clutches of the mind, that is, drop out of inner chattering.

You can do this by forcing yourself, but then again you miss. You can force yourself not to talk inside, just as you can force yourself not to talk outside; you can keep a forced silence. In the beginning it is difficult, but you can go on insisting and you can force the mind not to talk. It is possible. If you go to the Himalayas you will find many people who have attained to it, but you will find dullness on their faces, not intelligence. The mind has not been transcended, it has simply been dulled. They have not moved into an alive silence, they have simply forced the mind and controlled it. It is as if a child has been forced to sit in the corner and not to move. Watch him: he feels restless but he goes on controlling himself, afraid. He represses his energy, otherwise he will be punished.

If this goes on for as long as it does – in schools children are sitting for five or six hours – by and by they are dulled, their intelligence is lost. Every child is born intelligent, and almost ninety-nine percent of people die stupid. The whole education dulls the mind, and you can also do the same to yourself.

You will find religious people almost stupid, although you may not see it because of your ideas about them. But if you have open eyes, go and look at your sannyasins: you will find them stupid and idiotic, you will not find any sign of intelligence or creativity. India has suffered very much because of these people. They have created such an uncreative state that India has lived at the minimum. Paralysis is not meditation.

It happened once in a church that the preacher shouted at the revival, "Let all you husbands who have troubles on your minds, stand up!"

Every man in the church rose to his feet except one.

"Ah!' exclaimed the preacher. "You are one in a million!"

"It is not that. I cannot get up," said the man. "I am paralyzed."

Paralysis is not meditation, paralysis is not healthy. You can paralyze the mind; there are millions of tricks available to paralyze it. People lie on a bed of thorns: if you continuously lie on a bed of thorns your body becomes insensitive. It is not a miracle, you are simply desensitizing your body. When the body loses aliveness there is no problem; it is not a bed of thorns for you at all. By and by you may even start feeling comfortable. In fact, if you are given a good, comfortable bed, you will not be able to sleep on it. This is paralyzing the body.

There are similar methods to paralyze the mind. You can fast. Then the mind goes on saying that the body is hungry but you don't supply food, you don't listen to the mind. By and by the mind becomes dull. The body goes on feeling the hunger but the mind does not report it, because what is the point? There is nobody to listen, there is nobody to respond. Then a certain paralysis happens in the mind. Many people who go on long fasts think they have attained meditation. It is not meditation, it is just low energy, paralysis, insensitivity. They are moving like dead corpses, they are not alive.

Remember, meditation will bring you more and more intelligence, infinite intelligence, a radiant intelligence. Meditation will make you more alive and sensitive; your life will become richer.

Look at the ascetics: their life has become almost as if it is not life. These people are not meditators. They may be masochists, torturing themselves and enjoying the torture. The mind is very cunning, it goes on doing things and rationalizing them. Ordinarily you are violent towards others. But mind is very cunning: it can learn nonviolence, it can preach nonviolence. Then it becomes violent towards itself, and the violence that you do to your own self is respected by people because they have an idea that to be an ascetic is to be religious. That is sheer nonsense.

Existence is not an ascetic, otherwise there would be no flowers, there would be no green trees, only deserts. God is not an ascetic, otherwise there would be no song in life, no dance in life, only cemeteries and cemeteries. God is not an ascetic, God enjoys life. God is more epicurean than you can imagine. If you think about God, think in terms of Epicurus. Godliness is a constant search for more and more happiness, joy, ecstasy, remember that.

But mind is very cunning: it can rationalize paralysis as meditation, it can rationalize dullness as transcendence, it can rationalize deadness as renunciation. Watch out! Always remember that if you are moving in the right direction, you will go on flowering. Much fragrance will come out of you and you will be creative. And you will be sensitive to life, to love, and to everything that existence makes available to you.

Have a very penetrating eye inside your mind, see what its motivations are. When you do something immediately look for the motivation, because if you miss the motivation, the mind goes on befooling you and goes on saying that something else was the motivation. For example, you come home angry and you beat your child. The mind will say, "It is just for his own sake, to make him behave." This is a rationalization. Go deeper: you were angry and you wanted somebody with whom you could be angry. You could not be angry with the boss in the office, he is too strong for that, and it is risky and economically dangerous. No, you needed somebody helpless. Now this child is perfectly helpless, he depends on you. He cannot react, he cannot do anything; he cannot pay you back in the same coin. You cannot find a more perfect victim.

Look: are you angry? If you are angry, then the mind is befooling you. The mind goes on befooling you twenty-four hours a day, and you cooperate with it. Then in the end you are in misery, you land in hell. Watch every moment for the right motivation. If you can find the right motivation, the mind will become more and more incapable of deceiving you. And the further away you are from deception, the more you will be capable of moving beyond mind, the more you will become a master.

I have heard:

A scientist was saying to his friend, "I don't see why you insisted that your wife wear a chastity belt while we were away at the convention. After all, between us, as old buddies, with Emma's face and figure, who would?"

"I know, I know," replied the other. "But when I get back home, I can always say I lost the key."

Look: watch for the unconscious motivation. The mind goes on bullying you and bossing you because you are not capable of seeing its real motivations. Once a person becomes capable of seeing real motivations, meditation is very close because then the mind no longer has a grip on you.

The mind is a mechanism, it has no intelligence. The mind is a bio-computer. How can it have any intelligence? It has skill but it has no intelligence, it has a functional utility but it has no awareness. It is a robot. It works well, but don't listen to it too much because then you will lose your inner intelligence. Then it is as if you are asking a machine to guide you, lead you. You are asking a machine which has nothing original in it – cannot have. Not a single thought in the mind is ever original, it is always a repetition. Watch: whenever mind says something, see that it is again putting you into a routine. Try to do something new and the mind will have less of a grip on you.

People who are in some way creative are always easily transformed into meditators, and people who are uncreative in their life are the most difficult. If you live a repetitive life the mind has too much control over you: you cannot move away from it, you are afraid. Do something new every day. Don't listen to the old routine. In fact, if the mind says something, tell it, "We have always been doing this. Now let me do something else."

Even small changes: in the way you have always been behaving with your wife, just small changes; in the way you always walk, just small changes; the way you always talk, small changes, and you will find that the mind is losing its grip on you. You are becoming a little freer.

Creative persons get more easily into meditation and go deeper. Poets, painters, musicians, dancers, can get into meditation more easily than businessmen. They live a routine life, absolutely uncreative.

I have heard about a father who was giving advice to his son. The father, a noted playboy in his younger days, was discussing his son's forthcoming marriage.

"My boy," he said, "I have got just two pieces of advice to give you. Make it a point to reserve the right to one night a week out with the boys."

He paused. His son asked for the second piece of advice and then he said, "Don't waste it on the boys!"

He is transferring his own routine, his own ways to his son. The old mind goes on giving advice to the present consciousness: the father giving advice to the son.

Each moment you are new, reborn. Consciousness is never old. Consciousness is always the son and the mind is always the father. The mind is never new and the consciousness is never old, and the mind goes on advising the son. The father will create the same pattern in the son, then the son will repeat the same thing.

You have lived in a certain way up to now, don't you want to live in a different way? You have thought in a certain way up to now, don't you want some new glimpses in your being? Then be alert and don't listen to the mind. Mind is your past constantly trying to control your present and your future. It is the dead past which goes on controlling the alive present. Just become alert about it.

But what is the way? How does the mind go on doing it? The mind does it with this method. It says, "If you don't listen to me, you will not be as efficient as I am. If you do an old thing you can be more efficient because you have done it before. If you do a new thing you cannot be so efficient." The mind goes on talking like an economist, an efficiency expert. It goes on saying, "This is easier to do. Why do it the hard way? This is the way of least resistance."

Remember, whenever you have two things, two alternatives, choose the new one, choose the harder, choose the one in which more awareness will be needed. At the cost of efficiency, always choose awareness and you will create the situation in which meditation will become possible. These are all just situations. Meditation will happen. I am not saying that just by doing them you will get to meditation, but they will be helpful. They will create the necessary situation in you without which meditation cannot happen.

Be less efficient but more creative. Let that be the motto. Don't be bothered too much about utilitarian ends. Rather, constantly remember that you are not here in life to become a commodity. You are not here to become a utility – that is below dignity. You are not here just to become more and more efficient. You are here to become more and more alive, you are here to become more and more intelligent, you are here to become more and more happy, ecstatically happy. But then that is totally different from the ways of the mind.

A woman received a report from the school:

"Your little boy is very intelligent," said the teacher's note accompanying the report card, "but he spends entirely too much time playing with the girls. However, I am working on a plan to break him of the habit."

The mother signed the report and sent it back with this note: "Let me know if it works, and I will try it out on his father."

People are constantly searching for cues to control others, cues which can give you more profit, "profitable cues." If you are after cues on how to control others, you will be in the control of the mind always. Forget about controlling anybody.

Once you drop the idea of controlling others – husband or wife, son or father, friend or foe – once you drop the idea of controlling others, the mind cannot have the same grip on you because it becomes useless.

It is useful in controlling the world, it is useful in controlling society. A politician cannot meditate – impossible – even more impossible than for a businessman. A politician is at the very other end. He cannot meditate. Sometimes politicians come to me: they are interested in meditation but not exactly in meditation – they are too tense and they want a want a certain relaxation. They come to me and they ask if I can help them, because their work is such that they are too tense, and constant conflict, leg-pulling, rat-racing, continues. They ask for something so that they can have a little peace. I tell them that it is impossible, they cannot meditate.

The ambitious mind cannot meditate because the basic foundation of meditation is to be non-ambitious. Ambition means the effort to control others. That is what politics is: the effort to control the whole world. If you want to control others you will have to listen to the mind, because the mind enjoys violence very much.

And you cannot try new things, they are too risky. You have to try the old things again and again. If you listen to the lessons of history, they are amazing.

In 1917 Russia went through a great revolution, one of the greatest in history – but somehow the revolution failed. When the communists came into power, they became almost like the czars – worse, even. Stalin proved more terrible than Ivan the Terrible: he killed millions of people. What happened? Once they came into power, to do something new was too risky; it might not work. It had never worked before, "So who knows? Try the old methods which have always been useful." They had to learn from the czars.

Every revolution fails because once a certain group of politicians comes into power it has to use the same methods. The mind is never for the new, it is always for the old. If you want to control others you will not be able to meditate. About that one point, be absolutely certain.

The mind lives in a sort of sleep, it lives in a sort of unconscious state. You become conscious only very rarely. If your life is in tremendous danger you become conscious; otherwise you are not conscious. The mind goes on moving, sleepy. Stand by the side of the road and watch people and you will see shadows of dreams on their faces. Somebody is talking to himself, making gestures. If you look at him you will be able to see that he is somewhere else, not here on the road. It is as if people are moving in deep sleep.

Somnambulism is the state of the ordinary mind. If you want to become a meditator you have to drop this sleepy habit of doing things. Walk, but be alert. Dig a hole, but be alert. Eat, but while eating don't do anything – just eat. Each bite should be taken with deep alertness, chew it with alertness. Don't allow yourself to run all over the world. Be here, now. Whenever you catch your mind going somewhere else … It is always going somewhere else, it never wants to be here – because if the mind is here it is no longer needed. Right in the present there is no need for the mind; consciousness is enough. The mind is needed only there somewhere else in the future, in the past, but never here.

So whenever you become alert that the mind has gone somewhere else – you are in Pune and the mind has gone to Philadelphia – immediately become alert. Give yourself a jerk, come back home. Come to the point where you are. Eating, eat; walking, walk – don't allow this mind to go all over the world. It is not that this will become meditation, but it will create a situation.

The party was in full gear and a man decided to call up a friend and invite him to join the fun. He dialed the wrong number and apologized to the sleepy voice that answered. On the next try he got the same voice.

"I am terribly sorry," he said, "I dialed very carefully. Can't understand how I got the wrong number."

"Neither can I," said the sleepy voice. "Especially since I have no phone."

People are living almost asleep, and they have learned the trick of how to do things without disturbing their sleep. If you become a little alert, you will catch yourself red-handed many times doing things that you never wanted to do, doing things that you know you are going to repent for, doing things that you had decided – just the other day – never to do again. And you say many times, "I did it, but I don't know how it happened. It happened in spite of me." How can something happen in spite of you? It is possible only if you are asleep. And you go on saying that you never wanted it, but somewhere deep down you must have wanted it.

Just the other day, Paritosh sent me a beautiful joke, one of the rare ones, a jewel of the finest water. Listen to it carefully.

It was after the last war and a journalist was interviewing the Reverend Mother of a convent in Europe.

"Tell me," said the journalist, "what happened to you and your nuns during those terrible years? How did you survive?"

"Well, first of all," said the Reverend Mother, "the Germans invaded our country, seized the convent, raped all the nuns – except sister Anastasia – took our food and left. Then came the Russians. Again they seized the convent, raped all the nuns – except Sister Anastasia – took our food and left. Then again the Russians were driven out and the Germans came back again, seized the convent, raped all the nuns – except Sister Anastasia – took our food and left."

The journalist made the required sympathetic noises, but was curious about Sister Anastasia. "Who is this Sister Anastasia?" he asked. "Why did she escape these terrible happenings?"

"Ah, well," replied the Reverend Mother, "Sister Anastasia does not like that kind of thing."

Even rape is your desire; that too happens because you want it. It may look too extreme but psychoanalysts say it is so, and I also observe it is so. Without your cooperation even rape is not possible. A deep desire for being raped is hidden somewhere. In fact, it is very rare to find a woman who has not fantasized about herself being raped, who has not dreamed of herself being raped. Deep down, rape shows that you are beautiful, desired – desired wildly! It is said, it is a historical fact that when one of the most beautiful women of Egypt died, her dead body was raped, the mummy. If the spirit of that woman knew about it, she must have felt tremendously happy. Just think: a dead body being raped ...

You may deny it.

Just a few days ago a woman came to me. She had been raped in Kabul. And she was telling her whole story with such relish that I said to her, "You must have been cooperating."

She said, "What are you saying?" She felt hurt.

I said, "Don't feel hurt. You are enjoying the whole story." I said. "Close your eyes and be true. At least once, be true to me. Have you enjoyed it?"

She said, "What are you saying? Rape, and me enjoying it? I am a Catholic, a Christian!"

I said, "Still, close your eyes. It makes no difference whether you are Catholic, Hindu, or Buddhist, still, just close your eyes and meditate."

She relaxed. She was really a sincere woman. Then her face changed and she opened her eyes and said, "I think you are right – I enjoyed it. But please don't say it to anybody! My husband is going to come to see you soon. Never mention it!"

Just watch your mind: on the surface it says something, but deep down, simultaneously, it is planning something else. Be a little more alert and don't move in sleep.

The nagging old lady had been in bed for a week on doctor's orders. Nothing suited her. She complained about the weather, the medicine, and especially about her husband's cooking.

One day after taking in her breakfast tray and cleaning up the kitchen, the old man sat down in his den. She heard the scratching of his pen.

"What are you doing now?" she called.

"Writing a letter."

"Who are you writing to?"

"Cousin Ann."

"What are you writing to her about?"

"I am telling her you are sick, but the doctors say you will be okay soon, and there is no danger."

And then he asked, after a small pause, "How do you spell *cemetery*, with a *c* or with an *s*?"

On the surface one thing, deep down something exactly the opposite. He is hoping against hope, he is hoping against doctors. On the surface he will go on saying that she is going to be okay again soon, but deep down he is hoping that somehow she will die. And he will not accept the fact, even to himself. That's how you go on hiding from yourself.

Stop these tricks. Be sincere with your mind, and the grip that your mind has on you will be lost.

Now this small anecdote.

When wolves were discovered in the village near Master Shoju's temple, Shoju entered the graveyard nightly for one week and sat in zazen. This put a stop to the wolves' prowling. Overjoyed, the villagers asked him to describe the secret rites he had performed. "I didn't have to resort to such things," he said, "nor could I have done so. While I was in zazen a number of wolves gathered round me, licking the tip of my nose and sniffing my windpipe, but because I remained in the right state of mind, I wasn't bitten. As I keep preaching to you, the proper state of mind will make it possible for you to be free in life and death, invulnerable to fire and water. Even wolves are powerless against it. I simply practice what I preach."

A simple story, but very meaningful. The master simply went to the graveyard and sat there for one week, not doing anything, not even praying, not even meditating. He simply sat there in meditation – not meditating, just in meditation. He simply sat there. That is the meaning of the word *zazen*. It is one of the most beautiful words to be used for meditation: it simply means just sitting, doing nothing. *Za* means sitting – he simply sat there. And this sitting, when the mind is not there and thoughts are not there, when there is no stirring and the consciousness is like a cool pool of water with no ripples, is the right state. Miracles happen on their own accord.

The master said:

"While I was in zazen a number of wolves gathered round me,
licking the tip of my nose and sniffing my windpipe, but because I
remained in the right state of mind, I wasn't bitten."

A very fundamental law of life is that if you become afraid, you give energy to the other to make you more afraid. The very idea of fear in you creates the opposite idea in the other.

Each thought has a negative and positive polarity, just like electricity. If you have the negative pole, on the other side a positive pole is created. It is automatic. If you are afraid the other immediately feels a desire arising in him to oppress you, to torture you. If you are not afraid the desire in the other simply disappears. And it is not only so with man, it is so even with wolves. With animals it is also the same.

If you can remain in the right state – that is, undistracted, silent, just a witness to everything, to whatsoever is happening, with no idea arising in you – then no idea will arise in others around you.

There is an old Indian story:

In the Hindu heaven, there is a tree called *kalpataru*. It means "the wish-fulfilling tree." By accident a traveler arrived there and he was tired, so he sat under the tree. And he was hungry, so he thought, "If somebody was here, I would ask for food. But there seems to be nobody."

The moment the idea of food appeared in his mind, food suddenly appeared. And he was so hungry that he didn't bother to think about it; he ate it.

Then he started feeling sleepy and he thought, "If there was a bed here ... " and the bed appeared.

But lying on the bed the thought arose in him, "What is happening? I don't see anybody here. Food has come, a bed has come – maybe there are ghosts doing things to me!" Suddenly ghosts appeared.

Then he became afraid and he thought, "Now they will kill me!" And they killed him.

In life, the law is the same: if you think of ghosts they are bound to appear. Think and you will see: if you think of enemies you will create them, if you think of friends they will appear. If you love, love appears all around you; if you hate, hate appears. Whatsoever you go on thinking is being fulfilled by a certain law. If you don't think anything, then nothing happens to you.

The master simply sat there in the graveyard. The wolves came, but finding nobody there, they sniffed. They must have sniffed to see whether this man was thinking or not. They circled around, they watched, but there was nobody – just emptiness. What to do with emptiness?

This emptiness, this silence, this bliss, cannot be destroyed. Not even wolves are that bad. They felt the sacredness of this emptiness and they disappeared.

The villagers thought that this man had done some secret rites, but the master said, "I have not done anything, nor could I have done so. I simply sat there and everything changed."

This anecdote is a parable. If you sit in this world silently, if you live silently, as an alive nothingness, the world will become a paradise, the wolves will disappear. There is no need to do anything else; just the right state of your consciousness and everything is done.

There are two laws. One law is of the mind. With the law of the mind you go on creating hell around you: friends become foes, lovers prove enemies, flowers become thorns. Life becomes a burden; one simply suffers life. With the law of mind you live in hell, wherever you live.

If you slip out of the mind you have slipped out of that law, and suddenly you live in a totally different world. That different world is nirvana. That different world is godliness. Then, without doing, everything starts happening.

So let me say it in this way: if you want to "do" you will live in the ego, and the wolves will surround you and you will be constantly in trouble. If you drop the ego, if you drop the idea of being a doer and you simply relax into life and are in a let-go, you are again back in the world of godliness, back in the Garden of Eden, Adam has come back home. Then things happen.

The Christian story says that there was no need for Adam to do anything in the Garden of Eden; everything was available. But then he fell from grace and he was thrown out. He became knowledgeable, he became an egoist, and since then humanity has been suffering.

Each person has to come back to the Garden of Eden again. The doors are not closed. "Knock and they shall be opened unto you. Ask and it shall be given" – but one has to turn back. The path is from doing towards happening, from the ego towards no-ego, from mind towards no-mind. No-mind is what meditation is all about.

Enough for today.

Chapter 8

Life, Death and Love

? **Can you talk about facing the death of each moment and letting go?**

D eath is already happening. Whether you face it or not, whether you look at it or not, it is already there.

It is just like breathing. When a child is born he inhales, he breathes in for the first time. That is the beginning of life. And when one day he becomes old, dies, he will exhale.

Death always happens with exhalation and birth with inhalation. But exhalation and inhalation are happening continuously: with each inhalation you are born, with each exhalation you die.

So the first thing to understand is that death is not somewhere in the future waiting for you, as it has always been pictured. It is part of life, it is an ongoing process – not in the future; here, now. Life and death are two aspects of existence, simultaneously happening together.

Ordinarily, you have been taught to think of death as being against life. Death is not against life. Life is not possible without death, death is the very ground on which life exists. Death and life are like two wings: the bird cannot fly with one wing, and the being cannot be without death. So the first thing is a clear understanding of what we mean by death.

Death is an absolutely necessary process for life to be. It is not the enemy, it is the friend, and it is not there somewhere in the future, it is here, now. It is not going to happen, it has always been happening. Since you have been here it has been with you. With each exhalation it happens – a little death, a small death – but because of fear we have put it in the future.

The mind always tries to avoid things which it cannot comprehend, and death is one of the most incomprehensible mysteries. There are only three mysteries: life, death and love. And these three are all beyond mind.

So mind takes life for granted, then there is no need to inquire. That is a way of avoiding: you never think, you never meditate on life; you have simply accepted it, taken it for granted.

It is a tremendous mystery. You are alive, but don't think that you have known life.

For death, mind plays another trick: it postpones it – because to accept it here and now would be a constant worry. So the mind puts it somewhere in the future, then there is no hurry: "When it comes, we will see." And for love, mind has created substitutes which are not love: sometimes you call your posses-siveness your love, sometimes you call your attachment your love, sometimes you call your domination your love. These are ego-games, love has nothing to do with them. In fact, because of these games, love is not possible.

Between life and death, between the two banks of life and death, flows the river of love. And that is possible only for a person who does not take life for granted, who moves deep into the quality of being alive and becomes existential, authentic. And love is for the person who accepts death here and now and does not postpone it. Then between these two a beautiful phenomenon arises: the river of love.

Life and death are like two banks. The possibility is there for the river of love to flow, but it is only a possibility. You will have to materialize it. Life and death are there, but love has to be materialized – that is the goal of being a human. Unless love materializes you have missed, you have missed the whole point of being.

Death is already happening, so don't put it in the future. If you don't put it in the future there is no question of defending yourself; if it is already happening – and it has been already happening always – then there is no question of protecting yourself against death. Death has not killed you; it has been happening while you were still alive. It is happening just now, and life is not destroyed by it. In fact, because of it life renews itself each moment: the old leaves fall, they make space for the new leaves to come; the old flowers disappear, the new flowers appear. One door closes, another immediately opens. Each moment you die and each moment there is resurrection.

Once a Christian missionary came to me and he asked, "Do you believe in Jesus Christ's resurrection?"

I told him that there is no need to go so far. Each moment everybody is resur-rected. But he could not understand. It is difficult for people who are too much into their ideology.

He said, "But do you believe that he was crucified? Is this not just a myth, or is it a reality? What do you think?"

I said to him again that everybody is crucified every moment. That is the whole meaning of Jesus' crucifixion and his resurrection. Whether it is historical or not does not matter a bit. It is simply irrelevant to think whether it happened or not – it is *happening*.

Each moment the past is crucified, the old leaves disappear. And each moment a new being arises in you, resurrects. It is a constant miracle.

The second thing to understand about death is that death is the only certainty. Everything else is uncertain: it may happen, it may not happen. Death is certain, because in birth half of it has already happened, so the other end must be somewhere, the other pole must be somewhere in the dark. You have not come across it because you are afraid, you don't move in the dark. But it is certain: with birth, death has become a certainty.

Once this certainty penetrates your understanding, you are relaxed. Whenever something is absolutely certain, then there is no worry. Worry arises out of uncertainty.

Watch: a man is dying and he is very worried. The moment death becomes certain and the doctors say, "Now you cannot be saved," he is shocked. A shivering goes through his being, but then things settle, and immediately all worries disappear. If the person is allowed to know that he is going to die and death is certain, with that certainty a peace, a silence comes to his being.

Every person who is dying has the right to know it. Doctors go on hiding it many times, thinking, "Why disturb?" But uncertainty disturbs; certainty, never. This hanging in between, this being in limbo — wondering whether one is going to live or die — this is the root cause of all worry. Once it is certain that you are going to die then there is nothing to do. Then one simply accepts it, and in that acceptance a calmness, a tranquility.

So if the person is allowed to know that he is going to die in the moment of death he becomes peaceful. In the East we have been practicing that for millennia. Not only that, in countries like Tibet particular techniques were evolved to help a man to die. They called it *Bardo Thodol*. When a person was dying, friends, relatives and acquaintances would gather together around him to give him the absolute certainty that he was going to die, and to help him to relax, because if you can die in total relaxation, the quality of death changes. Your new birth somewhere will be of a higher quality, because the quality of birth is decided by death. And then, in turn, it will decide the quality of another death. That's how one goes higher and higher, one evolves. And whenever a person becomes absolutely certain about death, a flame arises on his face — you can see it. In fact, a miracle happens: he becomes alive as he has never been before.

There is a saying in India that before a flame dies it becomes tremendously intense. Just for a moment, it flares up to totality.

I was reading a small anecdote:

Once there were two little worms. The first was lazy and improvident, and always stayed in bed late. The other was always up early, going about his business. The early bird caught the early worm. Then along came a fisherman with a flashlight, and caught the night crawler.

Moral: You can't win.

Death is certain. Whatsoever you do – get up early or not – death is certain. It has already happened, that's why it is certain; it is already happening, that's why it is certain. So why wait for the moment when you are dying on your bed? Why not make it certain right now?

Just watch. If I say death is certain, can't you feel fear disappearing within you? Can't you feel the very idea – and it is just an idea right now, not your experience – just an idea that death is certain and you are calm and quiet. If you can experience it ... And you can, because it is a fact; I am not talking about theories, I don't deal in theories. This is a simple fact. Just open your eyes and watch it. And don't try to avoid it, there is no way to avoid it. In avoiding, you miss. Accept it, embrace it, and live with the consciousness that each moment you die and each moment you are born. Allow it to happen. Don't cling to the past: it is no more, it is already gone.

Why go on carrying dead things? Why be so burdened with corpses? Drop them, and you will feel weightlessness, you will feel unburdened. And once you drop the past, the future drops on its own accord, because the future is nothing but a projection of the past. In the past you had some pleasures, now the mind projects those same pleasures into the future. In the past you had some sufferings, now the mind projects a future in which those sufferings are not allowed to happen. That's what your future is. What else is your future? Pleasures that you enjoyed in the past are projected, miseries are dropped. Your future is a more colorful and modified past, repainted, renovated, but it is the past.

Once the past drops, suddenly the future drops, and then you are left here and now: you are in existence, you are existential, and that is the only way to be. All other ways are just to avoid life, and the more you avoid life, the more you become afraid of death.

A person who is really living is not in any way afraid of death. If you are living rightly, you are finished with death, you are already too grateful, fulfilled. But if you have not lived, then the constant worry continues: "I have not lived yet and death is coming. And death will stop all and with death there will be no future." So one becomes apprehensive, afraid, and tries to avoid death.

In trying that, in avoiding death, one goes on missing life. Forget about that avoidance. Live life. In living life, death is avoided. In living life, you become so fulfilled that if this very moment death comes and the future stops, you will be ready. You will be happily ready. You have lived your life, you have delighted in existence, you celebrated it, you are contented. There is no complaint, no grumbling; you don't have any grudge. You welcome death. And unless you can welcome death, one thing is certain: you have not lived.

I have heard one anecdote:

Two Hungarian noblemen fell into a deadly quarrel. But since neither was anxious to risk his life with either sword or pistol, a bloodless duel was decided upon. Each was to speak a number, and the one presenting the higher number would be adjudged the winner.

The seconds were of course at hand, and the excitement and suspense were extreme as the two noblemen, seated at opposite ends of a long table, bent to the task of thinking of a high number. The challenged party who had the privilege of going first thought long and hard. The veins on his temples swelled, and the perspiration stood out on his forehead.

"Three," he said finally.

The other duelist said at once, "Well, that beats me."

When you are afraid of death even the number three is the ultimate. When you are afraid of death, you go on finding excuses for how to go on living. Whether your life means anything or not one simply goes on finding excuses to prolong it.

In the West now, there is a craze about how to prolong life. That simply shows that somewhere life is being missed. Whenever a country or a culture starts thinking about how to prolong life, it simply shows one thing, that life is not being lived. If you live life, then even a single moment is enough. A single moment can be equal to eternity. It is not a question of length, it is a question of depth; it is not a question of quantity, it is a question of quality.

Just think: would you like one moment of Buddha's life or would you like a thousand years of your own life? Then you will be able to understand what I mean about the quality, the intensity, the depth. In a single moment fulfillment is possible, you can bloom and blossom: but you may not bloom for one thousand years, and you may remain hiding in the seed.

This is the difference between the scientific attitude towards life and the religious attitude. The scientific attitude is concerned with prolongation: how to prolong life. It is not concerned with significance. So you can find old people in hospitals, particularly in the West, just hanging on. They want to die but the culture won't allow them. They are fed up with just being alive; they are simply vegetating – no significance, no meaning, no poetry; everything has disappeared, and they are a burden to themselves. They are asking for euthanasia but society does not allow it. Society is so afraid of death that it does not allow it even for people who are ready to die.

The very word *death* is a taboo word, more taboo than *sex*. Sex has by and by become almost acceptable. Now death also needs a Freud to make it accepted, so that it is no more a taboo and people can talk about it and people can share their experiences about it. And then there is no need to hide it and there is no need to force people to live against themselves. In hospitals, in old people's homes, people are simply hanging on because the society, the culture, the law, won't allow them to die. And if they ask that they should be allowed to die, it looks as if they are asking for suicide. They are not asking for suicide, in fact, they have become dead corpses; they are a living suicide and they are asking to be got rid of it – because the length is not the meaning, how long you live is not the point. How deeply you live, how intensely you live, how totally you live, the quality ...

Science is concerned about quantity; religion is concerned about quality. Religion is concerned with the art of how to live life and how to die life. Seven years, seventy years or seven hundred years – what difference will it make? You will go on repeating the same vicious circle again and again and again. You will simply get more and more bored.

So change the focus of your being. Learn how to live each moment and learn how to die each moment, because both are together. If you know how to die each moment, you will be able to live each moment – fresh, young, virgin. Die to the past. Don't allow it to interfere with your present. The moment you have passed from it, let it be no more there. It is no longer there; it only goes on in your memory, it is just a remembrance. Let this remembrance also be released. This psychological hang-up should not be allowed.

I am not saying that you should forget everything that you know. I am not saying that all memory is bad. It has technical uses. You have to know how to drive, you have to know where your home is; you have to recognize your wife and your children. But those are not psychological hang-ups. When you come home of course you recognize that this is your wife. This is factual memory – useful, enhances life, facilitates it. But if you come home and you look at your wife with all the past experiences with her, then that is a psychological hang-up. Yesterday she was angry, now again you look with that memory in between, your eyes are clouded by that memory. The day before yesterday she was sad or nasty and nagging – now if you look through all these psychological impressions, then you are not looking at the woman who is right now standing in front of you. You are looking at someone who is not there, you are seeing someone who does not exist. You are looking at a ghost – she is not your wife. And she may also be looking at you in the same way.

So ghosts meet, and realities remain separate. Ghosts are married and realities are divorced. Then these two ghosts will make love, these two ghosts will fight, quarrel, and do a thousand and one things, and the realities will be far, far away. There will be no contact; realities will not have any connection. And then there can be no communication, there can be no dialogue. Only realities can love. Ghosts can only make impotent gestures, movements, but with no life in them.

Drop the past each moment. Remember to drop it. Just as you clean your house every morning, every moment clean your inner house of the past. All psychological memories have to be dropped. Just keep factual things and your mind will be very, very clean and clear.

Don't move ahead of yourself into the future because that is not possible to do. The future remains unknown; that is its beauty, that is its grandeur, glory. If it becomes known, it will be useless because then the whole excitement and the whole surprise will be lost.

Don't expect anything in the future. Don't corrupt it, because then all your expectations, if fulfilled, will make you miserable. You will not be happy about it because it is your expectation and it is fulfilled. Happiness is possible only through surprise, happiness is possible only when something happens which you had never expected, when something takes you completely unawares.

If your expectations are fulfilled a hundred percent, you will be living as if you are in the past, not in the future. You come home and you expected your wife to say something and she does and you expected your child to behave in a certain way and the child does. Just think, you will be constantly in boredom. Nothing will happen, everything will be just a repetition, as if you are seeing something which you have seen before, hearing something which you have heard before. You will continuously see that it is a repetition of something, and repetition can never be satisfying. The new, the novel, the original, is needed.

So if your expectations are fulfilled you will remain completely unfulfilled. And if your expectations are not fulfilled then you feel frustrated. Then you feel constantly as if you propose and God goes on disposing, you feel that God is the enemy, you feel as if everybody is against you and everybody is working against you. Your expectations are never fulfilled, you feel frustrated.

Just meditate upon your expectations: if they are fulfilled you will feel bored, if they are not fulfilled you will feel cheated, as if a conspiracy is going on against you, as if the whole existence is conspiring against you. You will feel exploited, you will feel rejected, you will not be able to feel at home. And the whole problem arises because you expect.

Don't go ahead into the future. Drop expectations.

Once you drop expectations you have learned how to live. Then everything that happens fulfills you — whatsoever it is. For one thing, you never feel frustrated because in the first place you never expected, so frustration is impossible. Frustration is a shadow of expectation. With expectation dropped, frustration drops on its own accord.

You cannot frustrate me, because I never expect anything. Whatsoever you do, I will say "Good." I always say "Good," except for only a few times when I say "Very good!"

Once expectations are not there you are free – to move into the unknown and accept the unknown, whatsoever it brings, and to accept it with deep gratitude. Complaints disappear, grumbling disappears. Whatsoever the situation, you always feel accepted, at home. Nobody is against you; existence is not a conspiracy against you. It is your home.

The second thing: then everything happens unexpectedly, everything becomes new. It brings a freshness to your life; a fresh breeze is continuously blowing and it does not allow dust to gather on you. Your doors and your windows are open; in comes sunshine, in comes the breeze, in comes the fragrance of the flowers – and everything is unexpected. You have never asked for it, and existence goes on showering on you. One feels godliness is.

The proposition "God is" is not a proposition; it is a statement of someone who has lived un-expectingly, without any expectations; who has lived in wonder. God is not a logical hypothesis; it is an exclamation of joy. It is just like "Aha!" And it doesn't mean anything more, it simply means, "Aha!" – so beautiful, so wonderful, so new, so novel, and beyond anything that you could have dreamt. Yes, life is more adventurous than any adventure that you can imagine. And life is pregnant, always pregnant, with the unknown.

Once you expect, everything is destroyed. Drop the past; that is the way to die each moment. Never plan for the future. That is the way to allow life to flow through you, and then you remain in an unfrozen state, flowing. This is what I call a sannyasin – no past, no future, just at this moment alive, intensely alive, a flame burning from both the ends, a torch burning from both the ends. And this is what let-go is.

? **A short time ago I heard you say that you saw yourself standing in the marketplace with a bottle of alcohol in your hand. Today I was refused darshan because alcohol was on my breath.**

This is from Vedanta.

What I say and what you hear are not necessarily the same. My alcohol is my alcohol, your alcohol is your alcohol. When I am talking about alcohol, I am not talking about your alcohol. I am talking about the alcohol of buddhas. Yes, they are drunk, drunk with the divine.

But I can understand. You go on hearing that which you want to hear. You don't hear me, you manipulate. You manage to hear whatsoever you want to hear. Your unconscious goes on interfering, it goes on confusing you. Yes, I said that I am in the marketplace and not only in the marketplace, but with a bottle in my hand. This is an old Zen saying.

Zen says that one who has finally understood himself comes back to the world – and comes completely drunk. But why a bottle in the hand? The meaning is clear. Not only is he drunk, he has something to offer to you also. That is the meaning of the bottle in the hand. If you are ready, he can make you also drunk – he has something to offer you. It is not only that he is drunk. He can share his drunkenness with you, hence the bottle. He has an invitation for you.

That's why he has come to the marketplace. You go to the marketplace to get something, he has come to the marketplace to give something. He has found something, and this finding is such that it has to be shared. Sharing is its intrinsic nature. You cannot keep your bliss to yourself: it is as if a flower is trying to keep its fragrance to itself or a star is trying to keep its light to itself. It is not possible. When there is light it spreads, it goes to others, it helps even those who are not prepared to take its help. The fragrance disperses into the winds for friends and for foes alike.

Once a man has attained, he has to share. Not that he has to do something to share it; he simply finds himself sharing – he cannot do otherwise. He moves to the marketplace where people are. Where people are stumbling in darkness, he brings his light to them; where people are thirsty, he brings his own drunkenness to be shared with them.

Yes, I am drunk and I have a bottle in my hand – can't you see it? – but it is not your bottle. People have an unconscious tendency to hear something which is not said.

I have heard one anecdote:

A cavewoman came running to her husband in the greatest possible agitation.

"Wok!" she called out. "Something terrible has just happened. A saber-toothed tiger has just gone into my mother's cave and she is in there. Do something! Do something!"

Wok looked up from the mammothian drumstick which he was gnawing and said, "Why should I do something? What the devil do I care what happens to a saber-toothed tiger?"

It is not necessarily that you hear that which is said. Your unconscious continuously colors whatsoever you hear; it continuously interprets in its own ways. The words may be the same, but a slight jerk to the meaning, a slight turning, and everything changes.

After ten years of marriage, a man was consulting a marriage counselor.

"When I first married," he said, "I was very happy. When I would come home at night, my little dog would race around barking, and my wife would bring me my slippers. Now, after all these years, when I come home, my dog brings me my slippers, and my wife barks at me."

"What is the complaint?" asked the counselor, "You are still getting the same service!"

Yes, the service is the same, but still, not the same. You may hear my words and you may think the meaning is the same. It is not, so please be careful. Handle my words very carefully; they are delicate. And before you decide what they mean, don't be in a hurry. Meditate. Otherwise not only will you miss, you may misunderstand, and not only will my words not be able to help you, they can be harmful.

? Is it possible for a politician to be enlightened?

Never heard of it, it has never happened. There are intrinsic problems. The very dimension the politician moves in is against enlightenment.

A few things have to be understood. Politics is a diametrically opposite pheno- menon to religion. A scientist can easily become religious. His approach is different but not opposite. He may have been working with matter, with the objective world, but his working is a sort of meditation. He needs a certain space in his consciousness, a silent space, to work and to discover. It is not very difficult to move from the objective towards subjectivity because the same space can be used for the inner journey.

A poet can very easily become religious. He is very close, very, very close, almost in the neighborhood. A painter or a sculptor can very easily become religious; they are already religious, unknowingly. They are already worshippers though they have not yet worshipped. They may not have thought about God, they may not have consciously been religious at all, they may not go to the church or to the temple, they may not be concerned with the Bible and the Koran and the Gita — but that is not the point. A painter goes on seeing something divine in nature: colors are divine for him. A poet goes on feeling something of the religious romance all around. All creative arts are very closely related — any moment consciousness can dawn, any ray can become a transformation.

But a politician moves in a diametrically opposite direction. His whole training is against religion.

I have heard an anecdote:

The congressman had delivered a stirring speech against a controversial bill. He was promptly buried in mountains of mail from back home as constituents wrote condemning his stand. Next day he was back on his feet in the house, this time making a speech in favor of the bill. When he finished, a colleague collared him.

"Yesterday," said the colleague, "you made an eloquent explanation of the principles which motivated your stand. I wonder, what has happened to change your mind?"

"Someday," said the congressman, "you will learn that there comes a time in every man's life when he must rise above mere principles."

A politician is an opportunist; in fact, he has no principles. He talks about principles, but a politician has no principles. He pretends that he has principles, but if he is a politician worth the name he cannot have any principles. Those principles are just to fool people. He is on an ego trip. He uses all sorts of principles.

I have heard about one politician. In an election campaign he was speaking in his constituency and there was a great controversy about prohibition: about whether alcohol should be totally prohibited or not. When he was speaking, a man stood up and asked, "What is your stand on prohibition?"

Now he became a little shaky because half the population was for it and half was against it. And he could see that half the crowd was for it and half the crowd was against it. Whatsoever he said was going to lose half the votes: if he said yes, then half, if he said no, then half. It was really difficult. He was in a dilemma.

And then he said, "You are all my friends. Please raise their hands those who are in favor and those who are against." Half the people raised their hands in favor, and half against.

Then he said, "Good. I am with my friends, I am all for my friends. You are all my friends and I am for you."

Now he is neither saying yes nor saying no.

The trip is of the ego: how to become more powerful, how to control others. Religion is just the opposite. It is not in any way an ego trip. One has to lose his ego. And one is not trying to be powerful, in fact, one is trying to understand the total helplessness of the part against the whole. One is learning how to surrender, not how to conquer; and one is not concerned with others, one is totally concerned with himself. If this much is possible, that, "I can become aware of my own being" – enough, more than enough.

The politician is concerned with the outside world, he is an extrovert. The religious person is an introvert. He is not concerned with things, with the world, with situations; he is concerned with the quality of his consciousness. A religious person is trying to find out how to be fulfilled; a politician is trying to show to the world that he is somebody. He may not be fulfilled but he pretends that he is fulfilled; the politician has opted for pretensions, hypocrisy. He simply wants the whole world to know that he is somebody; special, extraordinary, very happy. Deep inside he may be carrying a hell, but he believes that if he can fool everybody else, he will be able to fool himself.

That dream is never fulfilled. You can fool everybody else by smiling a false smile, but how can you fool yourself? Deep down you know that everything is getting cold and dead; deep down you know that everything is empty, in vain. But one goes on thinking, "If I can convince everybody else that I am somebody, then somehow I will be able to convince myself that I am somebody."

The politician is a liar. He is trying to lie to himself and to the whole world. The religious dimension is the dimension of being true, authentic.

Once it happened that a man entered a bar and said, "Bartender, I want you to meet my dog. He talks. I will sell him to you for only ten dollars."

"Who do you think you are kidding?" said the bartender.

The dog, tears in his eyes, looked up. "Please buy me," he said. "This man treats me cruelly. He never gives me a bone. He never bathes me. He is always kicking me around. And once I was the richest trick-dog in the country. I performed before presidents and kings. My name was in the papers every day, and ... "

"So he does talk," said the bartender. "But why sell a valuable dog like that for only ten dollars?"

"Because," said the customer, "I hate liars."

A politician is a liar, and he is trying to convince himself through convincing others.

A politician is almost mad – mad for power. Many people are in the mad-houses in the world. Somebody thinks he is Adolf Hitler, somebody thinks he is Napoleon, somebody thinks he is Ford or Mao Zedong. And they are in the jails, or in the madhouses, or in the hospitals, because we think they have gone mad. Somebody thinking that he is Adolf Hitler is thought to be mad, but what about Adolf Hitler himself? The only difference is this: that this man, this madman who thinks himself to be Adolf Hitler, has not been able to prove it, that's all. He is innocent. His madness is just innocence. Adolf Hitler, who proved to the world that, yes, he is Adolf Hitler is more mad than this man. His madness was such that he proved to the whole world that he is somebody: if he cannot create, then he can destroy.

There are only two possibilities. Either you can be a creator, and then you will feel a certain fulfillment that comes to a mother when she gives birth to a child, or that comes to a poet when poetry is born, or to a sculptor when he has created something – a beautiful piece in marble, in stone, in wood. Whenever you create something you feel enhanced, you reach towards peaks, you get high. All people who are creative are close to religion. Religion is the greatest creativity because it is an effort to give birth to yourself, to become a father and mother to yourself, to be born again, to be reborn through meditation, through awareness. A poem is good, a painting is good, but when you give birth to your own consciousness, then there is no comparison. Then you have given birth to the ultimate poetry, the ultimate music or the ultimate dance. This is the dimension of creativity. On the rungs of creativity, religion is the last. It is the greatest art, the ultimate art. That's why I call it "the ultimate alchemy."

Just the opposite is the rung, the ladder of destruction. People who cannot be creative become destructive because through destruction they can have a vicarious feeling that they are powerful. When Hitler destroyed millions of people, of course he had a very powerful feeling that "I am somebody, I can destroy the whole world." He was almost ready to destroy the whole world – he has almost destroyed it.

A politician is a destructive mind. He may talk about the nation, the country; he may talk about utopias, socialism, communism, but basically a politician is a destructive mind, and a destructive mind cannot become enlightened.

First, the whole energy should move towards construction, towards creation. Then only is there the possibility that by and by you participate in the ultimate creation that is nirvana, the ultimate creation in which you are born divine, infinite, unlimited. You expand, you spread all over existence. Then you are no longer a wave, you have become the ocean.

The politician can never become enlightened. I am not saying that the politician cannot move towards enlightenment – he can move, but as he moves, he will have to drop politics. A politician is also a human being, but he will have to drop the politics. By the time he comes to meditate he will no longer be a politician. Remaining a politician, a politician cannot become enlightened. His humanity is there: even a Hitler can become a buddha – some day. One hopes he will. Some day, far away in the future, even an Adolf Hitler is going to become a buddha; that is his potentiality. But then, by that time, he will not be an Adolf Hitler.

Nuclear war had come and gone. Only one tiny monkey in one isolated part of the world remained alive. After weeks of wandering about, he finally came across a little female monkey. He threw his arms around her in greeting.

"I am starved," he said. "Have you found anything to eat?"

"Well," she said. "I found this little old apple."

"Oh no you don't!" he snapped. "We are not going to start that all over again!"

Even monkeys are worried about humanity. And I have heard monkeys talking. They don't believe in Darwin, they don't say that man has evolved out of monkeys, they don't think that man is a developed form; they think man has fallen from the monkeys. Of course — fallen from the trees, fallen from the height, fallen from the monkeys.

And this is true in a way, because man has up to now remained political. The whole history up to now has been political; no civilization has yet existed which has been religious, not even Indian civilization. Not a single nation has come into being which is religious, only rare individuals, here and there, far apart — somewhere a Buddha, a Jesus, a Zarathustra, a Lao Tzu — islands. Otherwise, ordinarily, the main current of humanity has remained political.

Politics is basically ambition. Politics is basically wrong because ambition is wrong. You are not to become somebody, says religion, you are already. You are not to become powerful, you are already. You are extensions of God. You need not be worried about being powerful and being somebody on a throne; those are all stupid games, childish, very juvenile, immature. You cannot find more immature people than politicians.

In fact, in a better world, politicians will be kept in madhouses, and mad people will be allowed to move into the world. Those mad people have not done anything wrong. They may be a little off the track but they have not been harmful. Politicians are dangerously mad people, tremendously dangerous.

I have heard that before Richard Nixon renounced his throne, he called a meeting of his colleagues and he threatened that he had the power, he could go into the other room, push a button, and the whole world could be destroyed in twenty minutes.

And, yes, he had that power. Millions of atom bombs are ready, a button just has to be pushed. The power of the atom and H-bombs already made is seven times more than is needed to destroy this earth — seven times more. Seven earths of this size can be destroyed. We have become so skilled, super-skilled in destruction. And nobody can say, any day any president of America, or Russia, or China, can go mad. And politicians are almost mad — any day, anybody can push the button. And now it is only a question of pushing a button, and everybody has mad moments, angry moments ... The threat is very, very real.

Politics has been the disease of humanity, the cancer of consciousness. Drop all politics within you. And remember, when I am talking about politicians, I don't mean particularly those people who are in politics, I mean all those who are ambitious. Wherever ambition is, politics comes in; wherever you are trying to get ahead of somebody, politics comes in; wherever you are trying to dominate somebody — maybe your wife, or your husband — politics comes in.

Politics is a very, very common disease, like the common cold.

? Since I have been here, I have lost my ability to concentrate. It is hard for me to utter a logical sentence and I have become very forgetful. I feel myself as a stupid child. Is that the way to the intelligence you talk about?

The ability to concentrate is not something to feel blessed about. It is a frozen state of mind, a very narrow state of mind. Useful of course: useful for others, useful in scientific inquiry, useful in business, useful in the market, useful in politics, but absolutely useless for yourself. If you become too much attuned with concentration you will become very, very tense. Concentration is a tense state of mind; you will never be relaxed. Concentration is like a torch, focused, and consciousness is like a lamp, unfocused.

My whole effort here is to teach you consciousness, not concentration. And this is the point to be remembered: if you become conscious, any moment you want to concentrate on a particular problem, you can. It is not a problem. But if you become too focused with concentration the vice versa is not true: you cannot relax. A relaxed mind can always concentrate easily, there is no trouble about it. But a focused mind becomes obsessed, narrow. It is not easy for it to relax and leave the tension. It remains tense.

If you meditate, first concentration will disappear and you will be feeling a little at a loss. But if you go on, by and by you will attain to an unfocused state of light – that's what meditation is. Once meditation is attained, concentration is child's play. Whenever you need to, you can concentrate. There will be no problem about it and it will be easy and without any tension.

Right now, you are being used by society. Society wants efficient people; it is not worried about your soul, it is worried about your productivity. I am not worried about your productivity: man has already too much, more than he can enjoy, there is no need to go on producing more. Now there is more need to play around more; there is more need to be more conscious. Science has developed enough; now, whatsoever science is doing is almost futile. Now going to the moon is simply useless but tremendous energy is wasted. Why? Because scientists are now obsessed, they have to do something. They have learned a trick of concentration: they have to do something, they have to produce, they have to go on producing something. They cannot relax. They will go to the moon, they will go to Mars, and they will persuade people that whatsoever they are doing is tremendously important. It is absolutely useless.

But this happens. Once you become trained in a certain thing, you go on, on that line, blind – unless a cul-de-sac comes and you cannot go on anymore. But life is infinite. There comes no cul-de-sac. You can go on and on and on. Now scientific activity has almost become ridiculous.

Religious activity is totally different. It is not worried about being more efficient. The whole point is how to be more joyful, how to be more celebrating. So if you go with me, by and by, concentration will relax. And in the beginning you will feel afraid because you will see your skill disappearing, your efficiency disappearing. You will feel you are losing something that you have gained with so much effort. In the beginning it will happen. The ice is melting and becoming water. The ice was solid, something concentrated; it becomes water – loose, relaxed, flowing in all directions. But anytime you need ice, the water can be turned into ice again. There is no problem, just a little more cooling is needed.

This is my own experience. Whatsoever I say, I say from my own experience: the same has happened to me. First, concentration disappeared; but now I can concentrate on anything. There is no problem. But I don't remain in concentration; I can concentrate and relax whenever the need arises. Just as whenever the need arises, you walk; you don't just sit on the chair and go on moving your legs. There are a few people who go on moving because they cannot sit relaxedly – you will call this man restless! Legs in perfect order are needed so whenever you need, you can walk, you can run; but when there is no need you can relax, and then the legs will no longer be functioning.

But your concentration has become almost as focused as if you are continuously preparing for the Olympics. Runners in the Olympics cannot relax. They have to run a particular amount every morning and evening; they are continuously on the go. If they relax for a few days they will lose their skill. But I call all Olympics political, ambitious, foolish. There is no need.

Competition is foolish; there is no need. If you enjoy running, perfectly good – run and enjoy. But why compete? What is the point of competition? Competition brings illness, unhealthiness; competition brings jealousy, and a thousand and one diseases.

Meditation will allow you to concentrate whenever the need arises, but if there is no need you will remain relaxed, flowing in all directions like water.

"It is hard for me to utter a logical sentence ... " Feel blissful, feel blessed. What is the point of uttering logical sentences? Utter nonsense: make sounds, gibberish, like birds, like trees. Look ... !

[*At this moment a nearby tree decides, with the help of a passing breeze, to illustrate Osho's words by shaking its branches and causing hundreds of leaves to fall with loud rustling sounds to the ground.*]

This way! Is this logical? The tree is enjoying, delighting, simply shedding away the past.

Delight, sing, utter sounds, forget all logic! By and by you will become more alive – less logical of course. That is the price one has to pay. You become dead if you become more logical and you become more alive if you become less logical.

Life is the goal, not logic. What are you going to do with logic? If you are hungry logic is not going to feed you, if you need love logic is not going to hug you, if you are thirsty logic will tell you that water is H_2O, it is not going to give you water, real water, no, it simply functions in formulas, maxims.

Look at life, and by and by you will understand that life has its own very logical logic. Be attuned to it. That will become the door for your ecstasy, *samadhi*, nirvana.

" ... and I have become very forgetful." Perfectly good! If you can forget, you will be able to remember more. Forgetfulness is a great capacity: it simply means getting the past dusted off. There is no need to remember everything that happens. Almost ninety-nine percent of it is trivia. But you go on remembering ...

Just think: what do you go on remembering? Write it down and just look at it. It is trivia. What goes on in your mind? You will not be able to show it to your intimate friend because he will think you are mad. This goes on in your mind?

It is good. Forget. Forgetfulness is a great capacity because it will allow you to remember. It is part of remembrance. The useless has to be forgotten so that the useful is remembered – and the useful is very, very small, the useless is too much. In twenty-four hours' time, millions of bits of information are collected by the mind. If you collect them and remember them all, you will be mad.

I have heard about a man. He was once presented to the governor-general in India because he was a man of rare memory. He knew only one language, Rajasthani Hindi. He was a poor man, uneducated, but if you told him anything in any language, he would never forget it. He would repeat it like a parrot, not knowing what it meant.

He was called to the governor-general's palace; the governor-general was surprised to hear about his capacity. Thirty other persons were called, and in thirty languages they uttered a few sentences. It was arranged in the following manner: the man went to one person, the first, and the first person said the first word of a sentence. Then he went to another person and he said the first word of his sentence, in another language. Then he went to the third. In this way he went to thirty people. Then he went back to the first who said his second word. And in this way again – it took many rounds, many hours. And then he repeated all the sentences separately.

The governor-general was simply puzzled. He could not believe it. But this man went mad.

This much memory is dangerous. These types of people are almost always idiotic. Too much memory is not a good sign: it simply says that you have a very mechanical mind, it is not a sign of intelligence. Hence you hear so many stories of absent-mindedness about great scientists, philosophers. They are not people of great memory. Great intelligence has nothing to do with great memory. Memory is mechanical, intelligence is non-mechanical. They are totally different.

So don't be worried, it is good. The memory is relaxing, many things will disappear, space will be created in you. And in that space you will be able to become more brilliant, more intelligent, more understanding. Intelligence means understanding; memory means a quality, a mechanical quality of repetition. Parrots have good memories. Don't be worried about your memory. In the beginning it happens because you have accumulated much rubbish. When you meditate that rubbish starts disappearing, falling away.

" ... and I feel myself a stupid child." That is the way, the way to the kingdom of God. Lao Tzu says: Be like an idiot in this world so that you can understand the illogical ways of Tao. Jesus says: Be like a child – because only those who are like children will be able to enter into the kingdom of God. Don't be worried about those things; the nonessential is dropping away. Feel happy and grateful. Once the rubbish has dropped, the real will arise; with the nonessential gone, the essential will arise. This is the way to reach to one's own source.

But many times you will get scared because you are losing your grip on whatsoever you have valued up till now. But I can tell you only one thing: I have traveled the same path and have passed through the same phases. They are phases, they come and go. And your consciousness will become more and more purified, virgin, pure, uncorrupted. That uncorrupted consciousness is godliness.

Enough for today.

Chapter 9

You Have My Marrow

After·nine years, Bodhidharma, the first Zen patriarch, who took
Zen to China from India in the sixth century, decided that he wished
to return home. He gathered his disciples around him to test their
perception.
Dofuku said, "In my opinion, truth is beyond affirmation or
negation, for this is the way it moves."
Bodhidharma replied, "You have my skin."
The nun Soji said, "In my view, it is like Ananda's insight of the
Buddha-land – seen once and forever."
Bodhidharma answered, "You have my flesh."
Doiku said, "The four elements of light, airiness, fluidity, and
solidity, are empty, and the five skandhas are no-things. In my
opinion, no-thing is reality."
Bodhidharma commented, "You have my bones."
Finally, Eka bowed before the master and remained silent.
Bodhidharma said, "You have my marrow."

I can see clouds a thousand miles away,
hear ancient music in the pines.

Of what music have I been talking to you? The Hindu mystics have called it *omkar*, the ultimate sound, or even better, they have called it the *anahata*, the soundless sound, the sound that is uncreated, the sound that has always been there, the sound of existence itself. It is surrounding you, it is within you, without you. You are made of it.

Just as modern physics says that everything is made of electricity, Eastern mystics have said that everything is made of sound. On one thing modern physics and ancient mystics agree: modern physics says sound is nothing but electricity, and ancient mystics say electricity is nothing but sound.

It seems that if you observe the eternal music from the outside, as if it is an object, then it appears like electric energy. If you feel it introspectively, not as an object but as your very being, as your subjectivity, then it is heard as sound, *anahata*; then it is heard as music. This music is constantly there, you need not do anything else except listen to it. Listening is all that meditation is about: how to listen to that which is already there.

In a small school it happened that a small boy sitting in the rear of the classroom appeared to be daydreaming.

"Johnny," asked the teacher, "do you have trouble hearing?"

"No ma'am," he replied, "I have trouble listening."

I know you can hear, there is no trouble about it, but you cannot listen. Listening is totally different from hearing. Listening means hearing without mind, listening means hearing without any interference of your thoughts, listening means hearing as if you are totally empty. If you have even a small trembling of thinking inside, waves of subtle thoughts surrounding you, you will not be able to listen although you will be able to hear. And to listen to the music, the ancient music, the eternal music, one needs to be totally quiet, as if one is not. When you are you can hear, when you are not you can listen.

How not to be is the whole problem of religion: how to be in such a deep silence that being becomes almost equivalent to non-being – that there remains no difference between being and non-being, that the boundaries between being and non-being disappear. You are, and yet in a certain sense you are not; you are not and yet in a certain sense, for the first time, you are.

When thought is not disturbing you ... thoughts are like ripples on the lake; silence is like no ripples on the lake, just being ... suddenly you become aware of a music that has always surrounded you. Suddenly it enters from everywhere. You are overwhelmed, you are possessed.

This is the first thing to understand. You will not be able to know truth unless you have become capable of listening to the ancient music of *omkar*. This music is the very heartbeat of existence, this music is the very door of existence. You will not be able to enter the temple of godliness but with this music as the bridge. Only on this music, riding on this music, will you enter it. The kingdom of God is available only to those who have become capable of listening to the eternal music.

It has been heard, I have heard it. You can hear it: nobody except yourself is barring the path, nobody is hindering. If you are missing, you are missing only on your own account. There is not a wall between you and the music; even if you feel there to be a wall it is only your own thoughts, and even then the music goes on penetrating you. You may not listen to it, but it goes on massaging your whole being; it goes on nourishing you, it goes on giving you life, it goes on rejuvenating you. Your heart throbs in the same rhythm as the heart of the whole.

Whenever your heart falls out of line with the whole you are in trouble, you are ill. Whenever the heart is in rhythm with the whole you are healthy. Let this be the definition of health: whenever there is no conflict between you and the whole, not even a rumor of conflict, you are healthy. To be whole is to be healthy, to be whole is to be holy.

And what is the way to be holy, healthy, whole? Your heart should beat in the same rhythm as the heart of the whole; you should not fall out of line, out of step. It is a great cosmic dance, it is a great harmony. When you sit still, silent, not doing anything, meditative, prayerful, suddenly you start merging into the whole. You come closer and closer and closer and your steps are no longer heard as separate from the whole. You become part of this great symphony. Suddenly you are healthy, holy, whole.

How to come to this tuning with the whole? Why are you missing it? You are constantly in discord, you have many contradictions within you. Those contradictions go on like a tug-of-war within you, continuously, day and night, awake and asleep. You are constantly pulled into opposite directions. This tense state of affairs does not allow you to listen.

Even when you are in love you go on fighting. Even in love you don't fall in step with the whole. Even lovers go on fighting with each other; otherwise love can become a door to the ancient music. Hence Jesus says that God is love. If you love somebody, at least drop all conflict with him, or with her – with your child, with your wife, with your brother, friend, with your master – drop! But even there, conflict continues; a subtle way of fighting continues.

Because you are constantly in conflict within yourself, whatsoever you do is going to be an extension of the same conflict, a reflection of the same disharmony. This is making you incapable of listening.

I have heard an anecdote:

In Eastern Europe, half a century ago, when marriages were still arranged by marriage brokers, young Samuel had been introduced to the young woman of whom the marriage broker had sung a gorgeous hymn of praise.

After a short interview, Samuel motioned the marriage broker into a corner and said to him, in a furious whisper, "What is this woman you have brought me? She is ugly. She has a cast in one eye. She's unintelligent and she has bad breath."

The marriage broker said, "But why are you whispering? She's also deaf."

God is whispering. God is a whisper, and you are deaf, and God cannot shout. He is incapable of it because he cannot be aggressive, because he cannot interfere, because he cannot trespass, because he respects your freedom. He whispers and you are deaf. The whole of existence is a whisper, it is very subtle. Unless you are tuned, unless you have become capable of listening to the whisper, you will not be able to understand, you will not be able to hear the music.

And you have become very gross: you cannot even hear if God starts shouting. Jesus told his disciples, "Go to the house-tops and shout from there. Tell people what has happened to you." He had to tell his disciples to shout because people are deaf.

A great sensitivity is needed. To be religious is to be tremendously sensitive. And now comes the irony: religions have made you, on the contrary, more insensitive. They have made you almost gross by their constant talk of conflict, struggle, fight, ascetic methods; they have made religion also a battleground. Jainas call their *tirthankara*, Mahavira. Mahavira means "the great warrior" – as if there is a constant war with truth, as if truth has to be conquered.

No, truth is not to be conquered; you are to be conquered by truth. Truth ... just to think in terms of conquering it – it is absurd. You have to surrender to it. If you fight, with your methods, yogas, techniques, you will become more and more gross. You will not be able to feel subtle, delicate experiences that are constantly happening all around you.

Have you watched? If you are a musician your ears become very, very sensitive. If you are a painter your eyes become tremendously sensitive. Then you see colors others have never seen. Then green is not just green, there are a thousand and one shades of green. Then each leaf of a tree is different, has a different shade of green, is unique, is individual. If you are a poet then each word has its own romance; then each word has its own subtle music, a poetry around it. There are poetic words and there are non-poetic words. If you are a poet you become capable of seeing poetry everywhere: wherever you look, you look with the eyes of a poet. You see something else which cannot be seen except by you. Whatsoever you do, you become more sensitive about it.

Religion needs total sensitivity of all the senses – of the eyes, of the nose, of the ears, of the taste, of the touch – because religion is not a part of life, it is the whole. You can have a musical ear and you may not have eyes at all. In fact, blind people have better musical ears because their whole energy starts moving through the ears. Their ears become very, very sensitive because the eyes are not there, and eighty percent of your energy moves through the eyes. Eyes closed, the energy moves through the ears. Blind people become very, very musical. They start listening to subtle sounds of which you have never been aware. A blind person starts recognizing people by the sound of their footsteps.

I used to go to a blind man. Whenever I would enter his room he would immediately recognize me. So I asked him, "How do you do it?"

He said, "Because of your footsteps. Your footsteps are different from anybody else's."

Each thing is different. Just as your thumb impressions are different from anybody else's in the world – past, present or future – in exactly the same way the sound of your footsteps is different, unique. Nobody has walked that way before and nobody is going to walk that way again. But we cannot recognize people by their foot sounds, impossible.

The ear can be very, very sensitive; then you become a musician. If the eyes are very sensitive you become an artist, a painter, a sculptor. But religion is your total being, you become sensitive in all the ways possible. All the doors of your house have to be opened so the sun can come in and the sunshine can come in, so the fresh breeze can come in and keep you constantly alive and young and pure and vital. Be sensitive if you want to be religious.

What I am saying is almost the opposite to what you have been trained to look for. If you go to your religious people, the so-called saints, you will find them almost dull. They are not sensitive, in fact, they are afraid of sensitivity. They have been trying to eat food without tasting it, they call it *aswad*. They have made it a great method. Mahatma Gandhi used to teach his disciples, "Eat, but without tasting." Now if you do that, by and by you will lose the delicate sensitivity of your tongue. Then you will not be able to taste godliness. If you cannot taste food, how can you taste godliness? Godliness is food also, and in food godliness is hidden. The *Upanishads* say "*Annam Brahma.*" Food *is* Brahma. Now if you cannot taste food – you can dull your tongue, your tongue can become almost dead, you can simply go on stuffing yourself without tasting – then you are losing one dimension of reaching to godliness. Then you will not be able to understand when Jesus says, "I am your food, eat me." Impossible to think of it: you will eat Jesus also without tasting him!

Islam became afraid of music because music has tremendous power over humanity, and it is good that it has. Wherever religion sees that something has tremendous power over humanity, religion becomes competitive, jealous. Food has tremendous power over humanity. There are many people who live to eat and many who don't eat to live. Religion became afraid. Their God became jealous of food. A competition arose. They said, "Kill this sensitivity of taste, otherwise people will choose food rather than choosing God."

Music has tremendous power – it can possess. It can almost make you ecstatic, intoxicated. Islam became afraid; music was debarred. Music was thought to be irreligious because the ecstasy should come from God, not from music – as if music comes from somewhere else.

It happened in an emperor's court that a musician came. He was a very rare genius, and he said, "I will play on my veena, on my instrument, with only one condition: that nobody should move his head while I am playing. Nobody should move his body, people should become like stone statues."

The emperor whom he told that this condition had to be fulfilled was a madman. He said, "Don't be worried. If somebody moves his head, his head will be cut off immediately."

The whole town was made alert that if they came to listen to the musician, know well that it was risky: "Come prepared, don't move, particularly your head."

Thousands of people wanted to come. They had long cherished the idea of hearing this musician, and now he had come with such a dangerous condition, almost absurd. Who has ever heard of any musician asking for such a condition to be fulfilled? In fact, musicians become happy when people sway and their heads move and their body energy starts a subtle dance. They feel happy because their music is possessing people, their music is effective, people are moved. Emotion is a movement; hence the word *emotion*. It comes from *motion*.

When people are moved, thrilled, stirred, a musician feels happy, rewarded, appreciated. So what type of man was this? Only a very few people came, only people who were madly in love with music, who said, "Okay, at the most we can be killed, but this man has to be heard." Just a very few people came.

The king had made arrangements: soldiers were standing all around with naked swords. Then the musician started playing on his veena. For half an hour nobody moved. People were like yogis, sitting like stone buddhas, unmoving, as if dead. Then suddenly the people were possessed. As the musician entered deeper, deeper, deeper, a few heads started moving and swaying, then a few more.

When the musician finished in the middle of the night, many persons were caught. They were to be beheaded but the musician said, "No, no need to kill them. In fact, these are the only people who have the capacity to listen. Don't kill them. The others who have remained like statues have to be thrown out. Now I will sing only for these people. These are the real listeners."

The king said, "I don't understand."

The musician said, "It is simple. If you cannot be possessed so much that even life becomes irrelevant, you are not possessed. If you cannot risk life, then music is secondary and life is primary."

A moment comes when you can risk life. Then music becomes primary, then music becomes ultimate. Then you hear the ancient music in the pines, not before it.

But religions have killed your sensitivities. Hinduism and Jainism have been killing the taste, Islam the ear. And *all* the religions have been against the eyes. There are stories of saints who plucked out their eyes because they became afraid: eyes could lead them into desire, into passion.

In India a story is told about Surdas. He was moving through a town when he saw a beautiful woman. He became possessed. Then he felt guilty, so he went home and plucked his eyes out.

But eyes are not the culprit. In fact, to see a beautiful woman ... nothing is wrong in it. If you really see a beautiful woman and you have really sensitive eyes, you will see a glimpse of godliness there – because all beauty is it, all forms are it. Surdas goes on singing about the beauty of Krishna, but if Krishna's beauty is godliness, what about that woman whose beauty attracted him? By whom did he become hypnotized? Godliness is hypnotic.

Plucking out your eyes is a crime against godliness. If Surdas ever did it, then he is no longer a saint to me. He may be a great poet, but not a saint. But I have been moving deeply into his poetry and I feel somehow the story seems to be fabricated. It must be a creation of the priests, of the so-called religious, the mediocre, the stupid, who don't understand life. Otherwise every sensitivity leads to him, all roads go to him – where else can they go? If the problem arises it is not of the eyes, the problem is that you don't have *enough* eyes. Then a woman looks like a woman; you don't have enough eyes.

If it happens to you, my suggestion is clean your eyes. Become more sensitive. Train your eyes, let them be more and more pure, unclouded – and the woman will start transforming into divineness, and the man will become godliness, and the trees will disappear and they will be green flames of divinity, and the rivers will disappear and they will be nothing but constant flow of his energy.

All the religions have been against your senses, your *indriyas*. I am not against them, because my understanding is that whatsoever you are against, you are against godliness, because every door opens towards it and every path leads to it. Enhance your senses, become more alive in your senses. Let your sensitivity be total and from every dimension you will have glimpses of godliness.

Because of these wrong and foolish teachings, you are constantly in conflict within yourself. Because of these foolish teachings you love a woman and you also feel guilty because you love her – because somehow it looks like a sin. You love a woman and you hate her also because she is the cause of your sin. Of course you will take revenge. How can you forgive the woman who has drawn you into the mud, as the religious people say? How can you forgive her?

Listen to your saints: nobody seems to have forgiven the woman. Even after they have become great saints they go on taking revenge. Still, somewhere deep in the unconscious, the woman is lingering. They are still afraid. Then there is a constant fight, a quarrel, even in love – so what to say of other things?

Love is closest to godliness because in love you fall in tune with another being; in love you are no more a solitary instrument. A small symphony is created between two persons. Then the children are born and the symphony has more members. It is becoming an orchestra: children, family, friends. You are no longer alone, you have become part of something bigger than you. And this has to go on growing so that one day the whole existence is your family. That is the meaning when Jesus says, "God, my father." His actual word is not *father*, his actual word is *abba*; it is closer. *Father* also looks a little clinical, smells of institutionalization. *Abba, bapu* – they are so close, so intimate. A bridge has happened, godliness is not a faraway thing: "God is *abba* and I am his son. I am his continuity. If he is my past, I am his future. That is the meaning of a son: the same river flows.

If you go on growing in your sensitivity, a moment comes when your family grows and the whole existence becomes your home. Right now, even your home is not your home; even in your home you are not at home.

I have heard of an anecdote:

In some of the more remote sections of Tennessee there are still a few counties without any telephone. The Tennessee State Forest Service recently installed a telephone in one of these counties and linesmen tried to get a native to converse with his wife, then in a small town some thirty miles distant.

After much persuasion, Uncle Joe put the receiver to his ear. Just at that moment, there was a terrific thunderclap and the old man was knocked to his knees.

As he climbed to his feet, he turned and said, "That's her all right. That sure is my old woman."

Even in your home you are not at home. The very word *wife* creates some uneasiness in you, the very word *husband* creates some uneasiness in you. In Urdu, the word for husband is *kasam*. It also means "the enemy." The original root from where it comes is Arabic. In Arabic *kasam* means "the enemy" and in Urdu it means "the husband." Both are true, both are the meanings of the same word.

Even the people we love, we don't love enough. Also in our love, hatred goes on and on and continues. We are never one, we are never a unity; we are a divided self, divided against ourselves. This dividedness creates confusion, conflict, noise, and because of this noise it is difficult to listen to the eternal music.

If you go on continuously listening to this noise within you, by and by you completely forget that something else also exists by the side, round the corner. This inner noise becomes your whole life. The whole day you are listening to your inner noise – a feverish state – and in the night also you are listening to the same noise.

Of course, this noise goes on creating layers upon layers around you. You become almost insulated. You become like a capsule, closed from every side.

You don't live in my world, you don't live in your wife's world, you don't live in your child's world. You live in your own world, in a capsule. Your child lives in his world, your wife lives in her world. In the world there are as many worlds as there are persons. Everybody is closed into himself and goes on projecting things out of these noises, goes on hearing things which have not been uttered, goes on seeing things which are not there, and goes on believing that whatsoever he is seeing is true.

Whatsoever you have seen up to now is not true, it cannot be, because your eyes are not functioning as pure receptivity, they are functioning more as projectors. You go on seeing things that you want to see, you go on believing in things that you want to believe. Humanity lives in a sort of neurosis.

I have heard that once a man asked a psychiatrist, "In simple, everyday terms, without any of that scientific jargon, what is the difference between a psychotic and a neurotic?"

"Well," said the psychiatrist, after thinking a moment, "you could put it this way. A psychotic thinks two plus two equals five. The neurotic knows perfectly well that two plus two equals four, but it worries the hell out of him."

There are two types of people in the world: the psychotic and the neurotic. The psychotic has arrived, he has got the conclusions. He is the dogmatic person. He says, "Only *my* religion is the true religion"; he says, "Only *my* God is the true God." He's absolutely certain. He is very dangerous. His certainty is not because of his experience, his certainty is because deep down he is very much uncertain, in deep conflict, turmoil. How to avoid it? He clings to a conclusion, he will not listen to anything going against his ideology. He may be a communist or a Catholic or a Hindu or a Jaina – it makes no difference.

The psychotic person has already arrived, he has conclusions. He's no longer growing, he's no longer learning, he's no longer listening. He lives out of his conclusions. He, of course, misses life because life is a process, there is no conclusion to it. Life is always in the middle, there is no beginning and no end to it. And life is tremendously vast. All dogmas can have a certain truth about them, but no dogma is the truth – it cannot be. Life is so big that no dogma can comprehend it in its totality.

So a really intelligent person is hesitant. He's never dogmatic. He's ready to learn, ready to listen.

So many people come here. Whenever I see somebody who, while listening to me, is trying to compare notes with his conclusions, I know he's in deep trouble. And I can see from your faces whether you are comparing notes or listening to me. Sometimes you nod your head, you say, "Right, you are perfectly right, this is also my principle." You agree with me, not because you are listening to me – in fact you are happy because you feel I am agreeing with you. Sometimes your head says, "No." You may not even be aware of what you are doing, it may be just unconscious, but the gesture is bringing something from your unconscious. You say, "No, I cannot agree with this. This is against my conclusion. This doesn't fit with me." Then you are not listening. You are psychotic. You may not be in much trouble and you may not need a psychiatrist yet, but that doesn't matter much – it is only a question of degrees. Any day you can be in a psychiatric hospital. You are getting ready for it, preparing.

And then there is the neurotic person. He's continuously in conflict – he cannot decide even small things. The psychotic has decided even ultimate things. And the neurotic cannot decide even small things: what dress to wear today? Have you watched women standing there before their cupboards, so puzzled? They bring out one saree and put it back, and they bring out and put back – what dress to wear today? To help you out of such neurosis, I give you one color – orange. Free! No need to worry. No alternatives left.

Both are in trouble. The one who has decided for ultimate things: he has stopped learning, and the one who cannot decide for trivia: he cannot learn because he is in such a hell, such a confusion.

In my village, just in front of my house, lived a goldsmith. He was the sort of person you would call neurotic. He would lock his door, he would go a few steps and then come back again and shake the lock just to see whether he has locked it or not.

It had become a joke in the whole town. He might be in the market and somebody would say, "Have you locked your door or not?"

Now it was impossible. He would stop whatsoever he was doing; he would say, "Wait! I am coming," and he would run back home.

One day he was taking his bath in the river and somebody said something about the door. He jumped out naked and he ran towards his home.

I have watched him: he would come back again and again and again. It has become almost impossible for him to do anything else. The lock ... Just think about his misery.

Ordinarily, you are both. These are extreme cases: ordinarily you are both. In certain ways you are psychotic. You have decided the ultimate: that Jesus is the only son of God, the only begotten son. This is psychosis. Then what about Buddha and what about Lao Tzu and what about Zarathustra? In certain matters you have decided and in certain matters you are completely in confusion. A part of your being is neurotic and a part of your being is psychotic. And because of this madness you cannot hear the ancient music which is always there.

Meditation is to get out of your psychosis and to get out of your neurosis. It is simply to slip out of them so you don't have any ultimate conclusion with you on one hand, and on the other hand you are not worried about trivia. You are simply silent. You are simply being yourself, with no decision, with no conclusion, with no center, and not worried about small things. If you can be in a state where no thought interferes with your being, no thought passes by, suddenly you are overwhelmed.

Now this beautiful anecdote, one of the most beautiful in the history of Zen. And of course, it belongs to the first Zen patriarch, Bodhidharma. Bodhidharma is the genius of the absurd. Nobody has ever surpassed him.

When he reached China, the emperor went to receive him. Rumors had arrived that a great man was coming – and he was a great man, one of the greatest. The emperor went, but when he saw Bodhidharma he repented. He started thinking, "It would have been better if I had not come. This man seems to be almost mad!" Bodhidharma was coming with one shoe on his foot and one shoe on his head.

Even the emperor started feeling embarrassed to receive such a man, and when they were alone he asked, very politely, why he did this.

Bodhidharma said, "This is just the beginning. I have to prepare my disciples. If you cannot accept this much contradiction you will be incapable of understanding me, because I am all contradictions. The shoe is just symbolic. In fact, I wanted to put my feet on my head."

Bodhidharma took Zen from India to China. He planted the seed of Zen in China. He started a great phenomenon on its way. He is the father and, of course, Zen has carried the qualities of Bodhidharma all these centuries. Zen is one of the most absurd religions. In fact, a religion has to be absurd because it cannot be logical. It is beyond logic.

I was reading an anecdote. When I read it I remembered Bodhidharma. Listen to it.

A great zoologist informed a colleague that he was trying to cross a parrot with a mountain lion.

"No!" exclaimed the other. "What do you expect to get?"

"I don't know exactly," the scientist admitted, "but I will tell you this: if it starts talking you had better listen."

Reading this anecdote, suddenly Bodhidharma surfaced in me. He was the man who was also a lion. Ordinarily he would not speak, but his silence was also terrible and terrific. He would look into your eyes, absolutely silent, and he would go like a cold shudder through your spine. Or he would speak – then too he was like thunder. Find a picture of Bodhidharma and look: very ferocious, and still very sweet. A parrot crossed with a lion – very sweet and very ferocious.

The whole Zen discipline has carried the same quality with it. Zen masters are very hard on the outside and very sweet on the inside. Once you have earned their love they are as sweet as honey, but you will have to pass through hardship.

For nine years while he was in China, Bodhidharma sat facing a wall, gazing at a wall. He was known in China as the man, the ferocious man, who gazed at the wall for nine years. It is said that his legs withered away sitting and just looking at the wall. People would come and they would try to persuade him, "Look at us. Why are you looking at the wall?" and he would say, "Because you are also like a wall. When somebody comes who is really not like a wall, I will look."

Then one day, his successor came. And the successor cut off his hand and gave it to Bodhidharma and said, "Look this way, otherwise I am going to cut off my head."

He turned, immediately about-turned and said. "Wait! So you have come. I have been waiting for nine years for you."

After nine years he came back to India. When he was coming back, this incident happened:

After nine years, Bodhidharma, the first Zen patriarch, who took Zen to China from India in the sixth century, decided he wished to return home. He gathered his disciples around him to test their perception ...

... what they had learned from him and what they knew about truth. So he asked, "What is truth? Tell me in short." The first disciple, Dofuku, said:

"In my opinion, truth is beyond affirmation or negation, for this is the way it moves."
Bodhidharma replied, "You have my skin."

What the disciple said was true, but not truth. It was not wrong, but it was philosophical. It was not experiential, it was not existential. He said, "In my opinion ... " as if truth depends on your opinion.

Truth is independent of all opinions. What you think about truth is irrelevant; in fact, because you think, you will not be able to know what is. That which is can be known only when all thinking stops, when all opinions are thrown away, put aside. So I say true, but not truth; the opinion is not wrong, it is well-informed, but it is still an opinion. Dofuku has not experienced it himself. He seems to be of the philosophical bent. He has been speculating, thinking, weaving and spinning theories.

Bodhidharma replied, "You have my skin."

If it had been just philosophical, Bodhidharma would not have said even this much. But he said, "You have my skin – the outermost part, the very circumference of my being." Why? – because he said that truth is beyond affirmation or negation. Neither can it be said about truth that it is, nor can it be said that it is not. He has some insight. He has groped in the dark through thinking, logic, but he has come to a certain insight. And that insight is beautiful: nothing can be said about truth.

You cannot say God is, you cannot say God is not, because if you say God is, you will make God like a thing, as a table is or the house is. Then God will become an ordinary commodity, an ordinary thing. And then, as linguistic philosophers say, the table can be destroyed. Whatsoever is can become "is not." The house can be demolished. The tree is here today, tomorrow it may not be.

So what about God? If you use the word *is*, then what about God? Can God be in a situation where he is not? – because wherever *is* is used, *is not* is also a possibility. No, it cannot be said that God is. But can we say the opposite, "God is not"? That too is not possible, because if he is not, what's the point of saying "God is not"? What are you denying, and for what? If he is not, he is not. What is the point of denial? And people deny so passionately that their very passion says, "It must be, God must be."

Look at the atheists who say, "No, there is no God." They are ready to fight. For something which is not, who fights? Why are you worried? I know atheists who have been thinking their whole life and trying to prove that God is not. Why are you wasting your life for something which is not? For centuries people have been writing books and arguing and discussing that God is not. But why be concerned? It seems that God is, in some way, and you cannot rest at ease unless you prove that he is not, otherwise he will go on challenging you, he will go on calling you, invoking you. So to put yourself at ease you have to create a philosophy that he is not. This is rationalization.

And then God is so vast. Call it truth, as Bodhidharma would like. Buddhists don't like the word *God* and in a way they are right, because the word is so corrupted and so many people have used it with such wrong connotations, that it has almost become a dirty word. Truth must be both, because in truth existence and nonexistence must meet. Existence cannot be alone, it needs nonexistence by the side. Just as the day needs the night, just as life needs death, existence needs nonexistence. So the ultimate must comprehend both, that is what Dofuku said. But it is still philosophical; on the right track, but still philosophical, just on the periphery.

Bodhidharma replied, "You have my skin."

It happened that Pierre Laplace was a athematician, an astronomer, who in Napoleon's time wrote a ponderous five volume work on celestial mechanics. In it, using Newton's law of gravity, he painstakingly worked out the motions of the solar system in finest detail.

Napoleon, who fancied himself – with only partial justification – an intellectual, leafed through the early volumes, and said to Laplace, "I see no mention of God in your explanation of the motions of the planets."

"I had no need of that hypothesis, sir," said the scientist politely.

Another astronomer, Legrange, hearing of the remark, is reported to have said, "But it is a beautiful hypothesis just the same. It can be used to explain so many things."

To the philosophical mind God remains, at the most, a beautiful hypothesis; not a truth, but a helpful hypothesis which can be used in explaining many things; at the most, a help to explanation – just a theoretical need, not an existential need. When a philosopher talks about God, the God is cold, the God is not warm enough. You cannot love that God, you cannot worship that God, you cannot pray to that God, you cannot surrender yourself to that God – it is just a hypothesis. How can you surrender to the theory of $H2O$ or to the Theory of Relativity? How can you surrender, how can you raise a temple to the Theory of Relativity? Howsoever beautiful it is, it cannot be revered, it cannot be worshipped, you cannot pray to it. It remains a hypothesis, a tool in your hands to explain a few things which cannot be explained otherwise. But a hypothesis can be discarded any moment; whenever you can find a better hypothesis it can be discarded. Truth is not a hypothesis, it is a lived experience.

That is why Bodhidharma said, "You have only my skin." Skin goes on changing. Every seven years your whole skin has gone through change; you don't have even a single cell of the same skin. If you live for seventy years, your skin will have changed ten times. Skin is your outermost part, it can be replaced very easily; it is being replaced every moment. It is just the bag in which you are; it is not very, very essential. It is not your being, just the outer wall of your abode.

> *The nun Soji – the second disciple – said, "In my view, it is like*
> *Ananda's insight of the Buddha-land – seen once and forever."*
> *Bodhidharma answered, "You have my flesh."*

A little better than the first; deeper than the skin, is flesh. A little better, because this is no longer a philosophical standpoint, it comes closer to experience. But the experience is borrowed. She says:

> *"In my view, it is like Ananda's insight of the Buddha-land ... "*

Ananda was the chief disciple of Buddha who lived with him for forty years continuously, like a shadow following him. So the nun said that truth is like Ananda's insight of the Buddha-land — of that land of paradise, land of light. Once seen, it is seen forever. Then you can never forget about it, it is a point of no return. Once known, it is known forever; then you cannot fall from it.

But the experience is not her own, the insight is Ananda's. She is still comparing. Her answer is theological, not philosophical — theological, as a Christian theologian goes on talking about the experience of Jesus, and a Buddhist goes on talking about the experience of Buddha, and a Jaina goes on talking about the experience of Mahavira. It is secondhand, not firsthand; leaning more towards the existential, but still theological; more contemplative than the first — the first is more speculative, the second is more contemplative — better, but yet far away.

Then the third disciple, Dofuku, said:

"The four elements of light, airiness, fluidity, and solidity, are empty,
and the five skandhas are no-things. In my opinion no-thing is reality."
Bodhidharma commented, "You have my bones."

Still deeper, but not yet home. The statement is true but it is still a statement. The truth is said better than the other two, but it is still said — and the truth cannot be said. Once you say it, you falsify it. The very saying makes it false. He is right: the four elements of light, airiness, fluidity and solidity — that means the whole existence — is empty; there is no substance in it, it is just like a dream, of the same stuff as dreams are made, *maya*, illusory, nothing is reality. "Nothingness is reality" — right, but he is trying to say something which cannot be said.

Wittgenstein has said that it is better to keep silent where saying is going to falsify. Keep quiet if it cannot be said, because whatsoever you say will be a betrayal of the truth.

Bodhidharma commented, "You have my bones." You have come very, very close, but still missed.

Finally, Eka bowed before the master and remained silent.
Bodhidharma said, "You have my marrow."

"You have my very soul." Eka bowed before the master. That was his statement: bowing down in deep gratefulness, a gesture of thankfulness, and then remaining silent. This is the true statement, and it is not a statement at all. It is only through silence that truth can be said, because it is only through silence that the truth is heard. It is through silence that one comes to hear the ancient music in the pines. And only through silence can you say it without betraying it.

Eka did two things. He bowed down: that is a gesture, a gesture of deep reverence, respect, gratefulness, gratitude. That moment Bodhidharma could see an emptiness bowing down before him. There is nobody in this fourth disciple, Eka. He is just emptiness within. He is what the third was saying: emptiness, nothingness. He has the experience of what the second was saying: Ananda's Buddha-land. He is what the first was trying to utter philosophically: beyond yes and no.

Only silence is beyond negation and affirmation. Only silence is neither atheistic nor theistic. Only silence is religious, only silence is sacred. To show that sacredness of silence, he bowed down and then he kept silent. He really said it without saying it. That is the only way to say it, and there is no other way.

Bodhidharma said, "You have my marrow."

You have my innermost core of being.

> I can see clouds a thousand miles away,
> hear ancient music in the pines.

You can also hear it. It is your birthright. If you miss it, only you, and *only* you will be responsible for it. Listen in the pines ... just listen. In this very moment it is there. You have to be just like Eka: in deep gratefulness, in silence, it is immediately here and it has never been otherwise. A turning in is needed, *paravritti.*

Someone asked Buddha, "What is the greatest miracle?" He said, "*Paravritti,* turning in."

Turn in, tune in, and you will be able to see clouds a thousand miles away, and you will be able to hear the ancient music in the pines.

Enough for today.

For more information

www.OSHO.com

A comprehensive multi-language website including a magazine, OSHO Books, OSHO TALKS in audio and video formats, the OSHO Library text archive in English and Hindi, and extensive information about OSHO Meditations. You will also find the program schedule of the OSHO Multiversity and information about the OSHO International Meditation Resort.

To contact OSHO International Foundation visit:
www.osho.com/oshointernational

About the Author

Osho's teachings defy categorization, covering everything from the individual quest for meaning to the most urgent social and political issues facing society today. His books are not written but are transcribed from audio and video recordings of extemporaneous talks given to international audiences over a period of 35 years. Osho has been described by the *Sunday Times* in London as one of the "1000 Makers of the 20th Century" and by American author Tom Robbins as "the most dangerous man since Jesus Christ."

About his own work Osho has said that he is helping to create the conditions for the birth of a new kind of human being. He has often characterized this new human being as "Zorba the Buddha" – capable both of enjoying the earthy pleasures of a Zorba the Greek and the silent serenity of a Gautam Buddha. Running like a thread through all aspects of Osho's work is a vision that encompasses both the timeless wisdom of the East and the highest potential of Western science and technology.

Osho is also known for his revolutionary contribution to the science of inner transformation, with an approach to meditation that acknowledges the accelerated pace of contemporary life. His unique "Active Meditations" are designed to first release the accumulated stresses of body and mind, so that it is easier to experience the thought-free and relaxed state of meditation.

Two autobiographical works by the author are available: *Autobiography of a Spiritually Incorrect Mystic*, by Osho, St. Martin's Griffin (2001) ISBN: 978-0312280710, and *Glimpses of a Golden Childhood*, by Osho, The Rebel Publishing House ISBN: 8172610726

About OSHO International Meditation Resort

The OSHO International Meditation Resort is a great place for holidays and a place where people can have a direct personal experience of a new way of living with more alertness, relaxation, and fun. Located about 100 miles southeast of Mumbai in Pune, India, the resort offers a variety of programs to thousands of people who visit each year from more than 100 countries around the world. Originally developed as a summer retreat for Maharajas and wealthy British colonialists, Pune is now a thriving modern city that is home to a number of universities and high-tech industries. The Meditation Resort spreads over 40 acres in a tree-lined suburb known as Koregaon Park. The resort campus provides accommodation for a limited number of guests in the tastefully modern, silent rooms of its 'Guesthouse'; and there is a plentiful variety of nearby hotels and private apartments available for stays of a few days up to several months.

Meditation Resort programs are all based in the Osho vision of a qualitatively new kind of human being who is able both to participate creatively in everyday life and to relax into silence and meditation. Most programs take place in modern, air-conditioned facilities and include a variety of individual sessions, courses and workshops covering everything from creative arts to holistic health treatments, personal transformation and therapy, esoteric sciences, the "Zen" approach to sports and recreation, relationship issues, and significant life transitions for men and women. Individual sessions and group workshops are offered throughout the year, alongside a full daily schedule of meditations. Outdoor cafes and restaurants within the resort grounds serve both traditional Indian fare and a choice of international dishes, all made with organically grown vegetables from the resort's own farm. The campus has its own private supply of safe, filtered water.

www.osho.com/resort